SABRE PRATTLING

Andrew Rigsby is a former Royal Marine and a keen shooting sportsman. He has an active interest in reporting, investigating and writing about gun crime, and his first book, *Gunfire-Graffiti: Overlooked Gun Crime in the UK* was published by Waterside Press in 2012.

He regularly contributes to the media and has recently consulted on gun crime documentaries including Channel 4's 2022 *Murder in the Alps*.

The author has written on a variety of subjects, but his motivation for writing *Sabre Prattling* came from a desire to continue learning through over 40 years as a shooting sportsman, studying military history, collecting antique firearms and the fascination of language. He also brings his personal insight to this guide having had a career in the military and experience on operations and in conflict zones, which enabled him to see the destructive force of weaponry.

SABRE PRATTLING

THE LANGUAGE OF THE BATTLEFIELD

ANDREW RIGSBY

BEACHY BOOKS

First published by
Beachy Books in 2022
(an imprint of Beachy Books Limited)
www.beachybooks.com

1

A CIP catalogue record for this book is available from the
British Library.

ISBN: 9781913894078

Set in Sabon LT Pro

*Dedicated to my friends, family and colleagues.
Thank you for your support, suggestions and sometimes
surprised looks. To members of the armed services past
and present wherever they have served.*

This is all your fault, lock, stock and barrel.

Contents

WHAT ARE WE TALKING ABOUT?

We have a tendency to overindulge with our language. We pluck out expressions and phrases that in a literal sense grossly exaggerate what we really mean or what is linked to our demands, endeavours or actions.

We are *starving* when we are *hungry* and *parched* when we are *thirsty*. We are *freezing* when we are *cold* and *boiling* when we are *hot*. We *run like the wind, get stuck up the creek without a paddle* and *go off like a rocket*. What is particularly interesting is how we describe our day-to-day adventures, routines and events as if we were carrying or about to use a gun or a bomb.

Angered and frustrated by events, we *go ballistic*, *drop bombshells*, *character assassinate*, *blast*, *blow away*, *blow out of the water*, and *shoot down in flames* when all we actually do in these particular instances is *chastise*, *criticise* and *ridicule*.

We use militaristic and warlike terms in the workplace, *developing strategies*, *tactics* and *plans of attack* rather than just plain methods to outperform opposition or competitors in the corporate world. Leaders can be *up in arms* and *on the warpath*. We form *task groups* to sell simple products and build *fallback positions* and plan *last lines of defence* to counter business threat and loss. We *attack* and *defend* ourselves; we *fight* and seek to *wage war*.

On the sporting field, especially with ball sports, there's a lot of *shots* and *shooting* going on. We might hear a *call to arms*, receive orders to *dig in*, *do battle* and plan *rear-guard actions*. Professional footballers get *called up* to represent their country. During the 2020 Six Nations Championship rugby tournament one of the commentator's favourites kept creeping in when describing the strategic positioning and space creation for a sprint to the touchline that left tactically-selected players poised to *pull the trigger*. NBC coverage of the 2022 Beijing Olympics were unhappy with some of the points decisions during a men's snowboarding event and declared the judges to have *grenaded* their credibility. Unconnected, another sports commentator referred to the young and exciting Swiss snowboarder Jan Scherrer as the *Jan-grenade*.

The English language is liberally populated with idioms, similes and metaphors associated with firearms and conflict going back to the 14th century. Today we use descriptive conversational terminology that can be directly attributed to weapons and the mechanics of war and their application, perhaps not always realising what we are referring to.

At times, we literally don't know what we're talking about. Some of us have our well-worn favourites; others regularly *go off at half cock* and sprinkle all manner of expressions on their narrative like salt and pepper on their food. Pick up any newspaper, listen to any news broadcast, trawl through social media, sit through a presentation on any subject and you will always see or hear an example.

Very few people in the UK (around 5%) have an association with firearms. Some who don't might even abhor the thought of using these expressions but naively indulge anyway. Firearms are restricted to the military, elements of the police force and licenced members of the public who pursue shooting sports. In the United States around 40% of the population legally own firearms, with the majority for personal protection.

The legal use of firearms is restricted within the UK by the lawful protective measures that control the need and any responsible interest. The eventual manufacture and development of firearms came as a result of inventors and technicians stretching their imagination and developing skills. For thousands of years the entire world had made do with simple edged weapons, stabbing devices and had launched projectiles in flight from the string of a long bow or crossbow.

Firearms changed all that dramatically and contributed to the wider issues of more general, technical and engineering developments over hundreds of years. The expertise learned from mechanical applications, tolerances, durability, and strengths has been applied to other fields. Whilst firearms are engineered tools designed to kill, they have been equally effective in helping to maintain the peace.

This book was prompted by my interest in history, particularly military history and firearms. I became fascinated with our liberal use of expressions, a weather forecaster warning us about *staring down the barrel* of an approaching storm, a wily politician unable to give a straight answer because he is *keeping his powder dry*, an entrepreneur about to *shoot a rival down in flames*, an employer advising staff members to *raise their sights*.

I have had, perhaps, the misfortune but certainly the shocking visual clarity of experiencing the sight of aircraft being *blown out of the sky* and *shot down in flames*. I have seen warships *in the line of fire*, *all guns blazing* and troops experiencing a *baptism of fire*. Those images were transmitted to me and remain as an indelible image in my subconscious. I suppose, rather ironically, that those literal experiences mean I rarely use these terms in my own day-to-day language.

I have included a selection of expressions associated with weaponry and conflict before the introduction of firearms, namely edged and strung weapons, along with examples including metaphors (a word or phrase used in an imaginative way to represent or stand for something else) such as a *loose cannon* or a *flash in the pan*; idioms (a word or phrase which means something quite different from what it actually says) such as *bite the bullet*; and similes (a word or phrase that compares one thing to another of a different kind) such as *built like a tank* or *went like a bomb*.

The chronology is presented in alphabetical order. The narrative in *italics* is how we have now determined the meaning and use of words or phrases and how they are used figuratively. For many of the terms and phrases referenced, many have different meanings and dictionary definitions but those not in the context of the battlefield have not been described here. And after I present a short meaning or origination of the word or phrase which may also include mention of the many shared expressions of the mechanics of firearms and explosive devices, of which I refer to where appropriate, such as *lock, load, battery, cock, hammer, barrel, cylinder, sling, pattern, percussion, port, eject, spent, recoil, lever, bolt, chamber, slide, swivel, magazine, cartridge, piece, pellet, cap, lug, scope* and *action*.

You will learn that much of the terminology we use within our language harkens back to the early days of firearm technology and conflict. For example, most native English speakers know that to *take a lot of flak* means to be criticised or ridiculed and they will use the idiom in the correct sense. Some will know that *flak* refers to anti-aircraft gunfire, but few will know it derived from German ground fire ordnance known as *Fliegerabwehrkanone*.

Sabre Prattling is not masquerading as an official catalogue; the historical study of language is far reaching and open for debate. Nevertheless, many examples are clear in my sights. But, importantly, I compiled it for fun and light-hearted education so there's no footnotes, simply a bibliography of references at the back. But, as is often the case with history, it's sometimes difficult to ascertain facts from fiction and stories passed down from one writer to another. I'm sure you may well note down terms and phrases I have missed out, perhaps even disputing my originations, and if so I'd love to hear from you. I'm sure any amendments and additions may well make it into a revised edition! But, if my book prompts argument amongst the academics that's fine with me—*I'm keeping my powder dry* and intend to *stay out of the line of fire*.

For those interested, next I present a very short history of the gun to help get your bearings on some of the terms used in the descriptions, but for those too eager to get to my language of the battlefield, I start with a well-used classic...

A Brief History of the Gun

The early history of the gun cannot be easily separated from its original propellant, the mixture commonly referred to as *gunpowder*. Latterly it was described as *black powder* because of its colour. It is a mixture of charcoal, saltpetre and sulphur. While the use of the simplest guns is well documented in Europe, the earliest gun records come from the Middle East. It is considered that the Arabs learned about guns and gunpowder from their eastern neighbours and most historians believe that the Chinese invented gunpowder and the earliest firearms. There is little doubt that cannons were the first guns utilised, cumbersome and crude affairs that were every bit as dangerous to the users as well as the targeted recipients.

The Swiss firearms designer and writer Colonel Rudolf Schmidt traced the earliest use of guns and gunpowder in Europe. Belgium apparently came on the scene in 1313, with England in 1327. Sweden was late to adopt in 1400 by which time all of Europe were involved and experimenting.

The basic cannon design was developed into a handheld version. These were also simple affairs, namely a heavy barrel made from either brass or cast from iron. Closed at one end with a small touch hole access vent, the weapon was charged with a measure of gunpowder through the muzzle followed by a separating wad and a roughly cast round ball of lead or iron, failing that, anything that was available. The charge was fired by applying a lit match cord to the touch hole.

As time progressed these firearms became a little more sophisticated and user-friendly and the matchlock was developed. The match cord was now held in the jaws of a simple sprung lock called the serpentine, which was released by a trigger. The serpentine arm fell upon a small charge of gunpowder held in the pan next to the touch hole which in turn fired the main charge. This now enabled the firer to hold, carry and aim the weapon more effectively and a wooden frame became an integral part of the design, namely the butt (or stock) and fore-end that now accommodated the barrel.

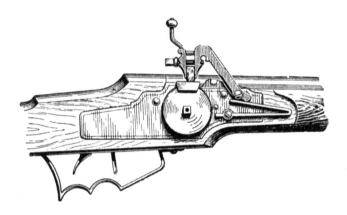

By the 16th century the wheel lock had been developed, a rather complex, intricate mechanism employing a coil-sprung wheel, which had to be wound up by a key and locked against a sear. When the trigger was pulled the locked, sprung wheel was released and it quickly rotated. This in turn was struck by some iron pyrites held in the jaws of a firing lock that descended towards and struck it, which created a spark shower that ignited the main charge.

A simple application of that ignition system still exists today employed in the Zippo cigarette lighter, the wheel being operated by the user's thumb and the resulting spark created by the struck flint, igniting lighter fuel rather than gunpowder.

The complex wheel lock was superseded by the snaphaunce in the mid 1500s and by the 1600s we had the early versions of the flintlock, an even simpler and more efficient ignition system but still based on the friction principles of the wheel lock to produce an ignition spark.

The term *flintlock* has become a generic expression and synonymous with antique firearms and any muzzle-loaded weapon is generally referred to by the layman as such.

By the early 1800s a Scottish Minister, the Reverend Alexander John Forsyth, had invented the percussion lock, which was a huge step forward in ignition systems, being simple, self-contained and completely weatherproof, doing away with flints and priming pans. He patented his detonation fulminate ignition system on April 11th 1807, but he didn't live to see the invention develop into the modern percussion system. From the mid 1800s more breech-loaded weapons became apparent along with self-contained cartridges.

Towards the end of the 1800s we had breech-loaded repeating and automatic weapons using a wide variety of actions. Today the technology focuses on improving the firearm designs that arguably peaked at the beginning of the 20th century. For 600 years a whole new technical language had developed, and it has kept pace with rapid changes in design and application.

ℒANGUAGE OF THE ℬATTLEFIELD

ℐIM HIGH / ℛAISING YOUR SIGHTS

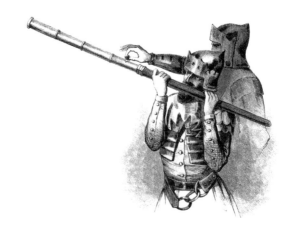

To extend a concerted effort to succeed in a manner that even short of total success might bring an acceptable outcome.

A bullet flies over a trajectory: a curved path that results from a decrease in velocity as it is forced to descend due to gravity. In order to strike a target at maximum range a weapon has its sights appropriately adjusted so that the barrel is elevated sufficiently and the shot aimed high so that the target may be struck towards the end of the curved trajectory path.

ALL GUNS BLAZING

Being resolute and with, perhaps, furious intent.

An exaggerated term harkening back to a tactical withdrawal or attack on land or sea where all available firepower is directed. Until the later part of the 19th century,

21

when smokeless propellants came into use, firearms and artillery used black gunpowder as a propellant. This compound produced a lot of flame and smoke, and it created a very visible and violent portrayal of conflict. Artillery barrages and naval cannon salvoes would have produced awesome and frightening scenes. *Guns blazing* would not have been an exaggeration. Modern weapon systems still produce flame and smoke but to a much lesser extent. This is a distinct advantage when you are trying to remain concealed. Modern military small arms will often have, what is referred to as, a *flash hider*, at the muzzle end, incorporated into the design.

$\mathcal{A}$MBUSH

To embarrass, publicly ridicule or verbally confront.

This is an old military tactic dating back thousands of years. Soldiers or combatants would lie concealed and in wait for an approaching enemy on ground of their choosing. The purpose of an ambush was to exert maximum damage to an enemy in the minimum amount of time and in a location that gave the ambushed parties little chance to escape, defend themselves or counter-attack.

Tactical ambushing became a very technical skill, and it is a method that is still used to this day. Contrary to what might be assumed as a result of Hollywood-type interpretations, a well contrived ambush is initiated by the ambush commander simply opening fire with his personal weapon to start the proceedings rather than shouting 'Fire!' and thus giving an unwanted warning to the enemy.

AMMUNITION

A verbal stockpile of argument, evidence, examples or opinions.

The contained ingredients that form what will be discharged from a weapon, be that a bullet, shot load or an artillery shell. *Ammunition* is separate from the weapons that discharge it, and it is matched very specifically. Ammunition must be loaded into a weapon; for a firearm this normally consists of cartridges, which are metallic tubes containing a propellant (gun powder), a bullet at the business end and a detonating cap at the base. Once the cartridge is fired the bullet is put into flight and the empty cartridge case is mechanically ejected from the weapon.

ARMED TO THE TEETH

Heavily or fully supplied with evidence or opinion.

This is apparently a phrase that originated in the Caribbean in the 17th century. It sought to describe pirates arming themselves with as many weapons as they could carry before boarding vessels. Carrying single-shot 'black powder' weapons along with axes and cutlasses, they chose, in addition, to carry smaller knives clenched in their *teeth*.

Assassinate / Character assassination

A character assassination can be described as a rigorous effort to discredit someone either verbally or in writing.

A political or religious killing often targeting an individual. In modern times generally carried out with a firearm but sometimes with explosive. Famous *assassinations* have occurred in history. Julius Caesar was assassinated in 44 BC. Four US presidents have been assassinated by firearms, the last being JFK in 1963. The Austrian Archduke Franz Ferdinand was shot and killed by Gavrilo Princip, a radical Bosnian student, which is considered to be the spark that ignited the First World War. In recent times, the Pakistan leader Benazir Bhutto lost her life to a gunman in 2007.

ℬACKFIRE

A plan, objective or proposal that goes unexpectedly wrong.

A more recent association to a firearm that might *backfire* if there is considerable weakness in the action or breech, or if the wrong ammunition is used. The rapidly expanding gas created from the burning propellant finds the easiest route out and this might be rearwards instead of forwards down the barrel thus endangering the firer. This was rarely a problem with muzzle-loaded weapons because the breech was closed off. It could, however, occur if there was a fault in a breech-loaded weapon. The term relating to firearms was apparently never used until World War I.

The origins of this expression are said to relate to the tendency for early internal combustion engines to *backfire*, that being the explosions that emit from an exhaust when fuel has ignited in it. People naturally not expecting to hear gunfire in a peaceful urban environment often describe a situation where, indeed, it has occurred as initially thinking the sound was a vehicle backfiring. The sound emitted can sound very much like a gunshot.

Another source of this phrase came from the firefighting skills that were developed by US settlers in the 19th century. They attempted to guard against grass or forest fires by deliberately raising small controllable fires, which they called *backfires* to remove any flammable material in advance of a larger fire and so deprive it of fuel. This literal method of fighting fire with fire was often successful, although the settlers' lack of effective fire control equipment meant that their own initiated fires occasionally got out of control and made matters worse rather than better. The method has continued to be used, however, and foresters globally now routinely create roads or unplanted areas to act as firebreaks in woodland or forest areas that are at risk of fire.

Ballistic / Going ballistic

To fly into a rage, displaying deep emotional upset or anger.

The study of *ballistics* is the study of projectiles. According to the Oxford English Dictionary (OED), *ballistic* originates from the Latin, based on the Greek word *ballein* 'to throw'. The *ballista* is defined as '*a catapult used in ancient warfare for hurling large stones*', but countless historical references seem to make it clear it was mainly for firing bolts, like a huge crossbow and it is recorded as being so. Roman writer Vegetius wrote in the Middle Ages of the *ballista* in his *Epitome of Military Science* (translated from the Latin), '*...Above all, it is equipped with ballista-bolts which no cuirass (breastplate armour) or shield can withstand...*'

It was one of many 'siege engines' including catapults,

slings, onager and trebuchet, to name but a few, that were built to wage siege warfare against castles and towns and people from Ancient Greek times to Medieval days. The Romans evolved the design following their need for a more compact siege weapon and the mobile ballista was ideal in their defence of Roman Britain against invading barbarians.

The two arms of a ballista were made of wood and ropes, acting as springs, and attached to each arm. Human hair or animal sinew was twisted to make the strands of rope. When the bow-arms of the ballista were pulled back, they twisted the ropes, and the bowstring was pulled back by a winch. When fired, ballista catapults could propel bolts, arrows and javelins far into the enemy with lethal effect.

Some sources state the idiom became more widely known during the 20th century following the development of ballistic missiles.

BAPTISM OF FIRE

A tough and demanding initiation at work or on the sports field.

The original phrase has its origins in the Bible, but in its military context Napolean Bonaparte hit the nail on the head when he said, '*When soldiers have been baptized in the fire of a battle-field, they have all one rank in my eyes.*' and then made the term popular with '*I love a brave soldier who has undergone the baptism of fire.*'

Military personnel who have gone through training, however realistic and detailed, can never experience the real numbing fear of being subjected to enemy fire until they are exposed to the real thing. The first initiation and the effect it can have on individuals can never, however, be accurately anticipated. The US senior army officer General MacArthur was alleged to have once said, '*Whoever thinks the pen is mightier than the sword has never encountered automatic weapons.*'

BARRAGE

An overwhelming outburst of criticism or comment.

A *barrage* is generally associated with artillery. Skilfully utilised, accurate and sustained artillery fire can have an overwhelming effect. Not only is it physically destructive, but the psychological implications can be devastating. Napoleon Bonaparte was an artillery officer who recognised the importance of this asset. Much use was made of artillery during the First World War, and the intricate trench systems were specifically designed to defend against it. The term *shell-shocked* (see **Shell-shocked** on page 139) came from this conflict. We have a more appropriate medical expression now: *Post Traumatic Stress Disorder (PTSD)*.

ℬATTLE

A commonly used expression describing a contest, the completion of a task or sporting competition. Battling

with competitors; the uphill battle of completing daily chores or unpopular duties.

Battle derives from 13th century Old French, *bataille*, linked to Latin, *battualia*, a term describing the '*exercising of soldiers and gladiators in fighting and fencing*'. A battle is a defined military engagement between two sides with the same ultimate objective. A *battle*, in this context, is an uncompromising, physically threatening encounter, anticipating loss of life. Perhaps, the closest we ever come to this, in real terms, is the *personal battle* we might have with the terminal threat of an illness or disease.

ℬATTLEAXE

A rather fearsome, complaining and unfriendly old woman.

The *battleaxe*, and variations of it, existed amongst the warrior class of many nations for thousands of years. This was a large and heavy handheld weapon used for bludgeoning and causing massive severing wounds. Weapons like the battleaxe, and other bladed and stabbing accoutrements, were still being used alongside firearms well into the 19th century. Native Americans used a fearsome version called a tomahawk, which they carried along with bows, knives, spears and firearms.

BAYONET FIT

A type of twist lug light bulb fit.

The *bayonet* design originated in the 18th century as a means for military firearms to secure a sword-like blade to the muzzle of a musket or rifle. This consisted of a sleeve that slotted over the muzzle and was locked into place by way of a Z-slot and stud. The city of Bayonne in southern France had long been noted for its cutlery and daggers from its workshops. This has resulted in a reference to the military-grade weapon.

In the mid 17th century military bayonets were simple devices, described by Jacques de Chastenet, Vicomte de Puységur, as a foot long with a tapering wooden handle that could be inserted into the muzzle of a musket. However, these early 'plug bayonets', whilst furnishing a soldier with another weapon, prevented the weapon from being loaded and fired. It was not until 1671 in France that Jean Martinet, a senior army officer, standardised the issue of plug bayonets to the French military.

BESIEGED

Overwhelmed with requests; an individual or group being surrounded by admirers, vilifiers or the press.

Besieging is a medieval military operation involving the surrounding of a town, castle or fortress by an army to capture or force a surrender. The term derives from the

Middle English word *assiege*, from the Old French *asegier* 'to besiege'. A *siege* was a tactic which initiated a waiting game, cutting off supplies as well as military actions.

The Middle Ages was an extremely violent era in history, littered with battles in both Europe and the Middle East. The quest for power led to invasions of lands and territories which had to be fought for. The Middle Ages was the era when great medieval castles were built, acting as a power base for the medieval kings, lords and knights. A new type of warfare—siege warfare—was waged to win a castle or a walled town or city, which called for a variety of different tactics, siege weapons and apparatus.

ℬIG GUNS

Senior management; corporate litigators; a planned last resort; a final all-out effort.

Big guns is a simple term used to describe artillery or naval guns, as opposed to *small arms*, which are the weapons carried by individuals. The use of artillery and naval gunfire support has often been recognised to be an integral part of an offensive or defensive operation. An offensive might be preceded with an artillery or naval gunfire bombardment. These *big* weapons might well be called upon to give support during the movement of an attack and give cover during a withdrawal or retreat.

ℬITE THE BULLET

Exposing oneself to a very demanding, unpleasant or difficult task.

Before the days of anaesthetics a patient would sometimes have to endure great physical pain whilst suffering a surgical procedure, and it is thought that military personnel might have been given a bullet to bite on to help their demise. That does seem rather odd and there is no documentation to support this. A leather strap would have been more practical and mention of that can be found. One theory is it might have derived from the hardship endured by Indian Sepoys who would have had to *bite the top off their paper cartridges* that were smeared with the mixture of sacred and offensive animal fat.

ℬLITZ

A very thorough, fast and focused culminating effort on fulfilling a task whilst paying fine attention to detail.

Blitzkrieg (from the German 'lightening war') was a military tactic of a fast and concentrated attack by aircraft bombing, artillery barrage and fast-moving armoured vehicles, in complete contrast to the slow attrition of World War I trench warfare. Though the tactic was employed by the Germans in World War II, the word, it seems, was invented by journalists. The first known use of the term *blitzkrieg* was in a 1939 American *Time* magazine article on the Polish campaign, but it is clear it was rarely, if ever, used in official German military campaign planning; allegedly, even Hitler disliked the phrase. Of course, the *Blitz* was a defined period in history when the German Luftwaffe bombed London between 1940 and 1941.

*B*LOW UP IN YOUR FACE

An exaggerated term for a plan or action going dramatically wrong.

Black gunpowder and early explosives were quite unstable and great care had to be exercised when handling, mixing or preparing them for use. On board warships gunpowder stocks were kept in special containers in magazines. In battle it was the job of 'powder monkeys', who were often young boys, to supply gunpowder charges to the gun crews. These youngsters wore canvas slippers to minimise the chance of sparks being generated. Modern propellants and explosives are far safer to handle.

BLOWING AWAY / BLOWN OUT OF THE WATER

A heavily weighted and convincing argument deservedly ridiculing a proven perspective.

Blowing out of the water was a seaborne inference which,

whilst an exaggeration, meant exactly as described, the total destruction of a vessel by gunfire. Whilst parts of a ship can be propelled skyward by force of explosion (out of the water), eventually a doomed ship will be overwhelmed by water and it will sink.

*B*LOWN AWAY

Can be the complete opposite and is used as a term of endearment. It is used to describe the favourable reaction of somebody who is hugely impressed by an action, a person, a feature, object or event.

Blown away by a gun was a particularly gory practise of military execution. The victim was secured in a standing position with the small of their back or stomach up against the muzzle of a loaded artillery piece or cannon. The weapon did not need a charge with a projectile; a blank propellant charge was sufficient. When the gun was fired the torso disintegrated. The area to the side of a gun was as dangerous to witnesses as directly ahead. Execution in this format was often perpetrated on religious grounds, being that a violent dismemberment jeopardised a recipient's path to the afterlife. Further discrimination and insult came as a result of domestic dogs and carnivorous wildlife feeding off the freshly butchered remains lying in the open.

ℬOMB / ᏩOING OFF LIKE A BOMB / ᏩOING LIKE A BOMB

Terms like 'going like a bomb' and 'going off like a bomb' are associated with a person completing a task very rapidly or moving very quickly under their own power or in some form of vehicle. Can also be likened to a sudden loud noise which is not actually linked to an explosion.

A *bomb* is an explosive device that takes many forms and a true explosive weapon that is many times more destructive and powerful than the implied term. Associated as an aerial-delivered weapon from recognised military sources and the weapon of choice for terrorist factions in the form of a planted device.

Clinically referred to as an *IED* (Improvised Explosive Device). From the early days of gunpowder large exploding devices were constructed with a view to destroying structures and inflicting death and wounds amongst large bodies of troops or people. *Going like a rocket* is a term used in a similar context as is *going like dynamite,* although we don't hear that expression so much these days. Dynamite is an early explosive.

ℬOMBARDED

Overwhelmed with criticism, requests, demands or, indeed, praise and adulation.

From the Old French, *bombarde* 'a stone throwing engine'. Used from the 15th century, these massive early cannons consisted of a barrel typically 8–10 feet in length with a bore of 15 inches and weighing over 1.5 tons. It was mounted on an oak firing sledge. The sort of missile it would fire would be a limestone cannonball slightly smaller in diameter to the bore, which might have been wrapped in lead. This missile would weigh around 140 pounds and it had a range of up to a mile. Bombards from this time were still being used over a hundred years later.

The term *bombarded* continued and is still to this day sometimes used to refer to the result of an artillery or mortar attack or bombs delivered by aircraft. The rank of *bombardier* in the Royal Artillery is the akin to a corporal in other Army units. The *bombardier* was also a crew task within a military bomber aircraft. Pyppes Dowghter is by far the largest working replica of a *bombard* that can be found in Britain.

ℬOMB DOORS

Electrical sliding doors giving access to a commercial

location, sports facility, training venue, etc. They may be described as such because it is the access point for visiting participants, candidates and guests who might be challenging, demanding or even perplexing.

Bomb doors are hinged doors in the underside of an aircraft fuselage that give access to a bomb bay for the storage of ariel bombs. Before bombs are dropped the hinged doors are opened; the sight is intimidating and a prelude to potential devastation.

ℬOMB SITE

A messy location, room, facility or living space.

Bomb sites were devastated urban areas that were common in some cities and towns all over the world after the Second World War. Many of them remained so for years afterwards. In the UK there were still bomb site locations within some of the larger conurbations in the 1960s, but over time they have been cleared and redeveloped. Unexploded devices still turn up during excavation processes. How often did your parents describe your bedroom as a *bomb site*?

ℬOMBSHELL

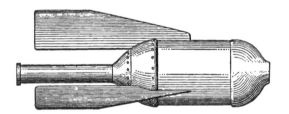

To deliver or drop an unexpected declaration, announcement or ultimatum. A blonde, provocative and sexually alluring female may be described as a 'blonde bombshell'.

A bomb is usually associated with the type of explosive weapon that is dropped from an aircraft. A mortar round

45

is also referred to as a bomb, because it has a very high delivery trajectory and eventually falls onto its target in the same way. The *bombshell* is simply the metal casing that surrounds the explosive element of an aircraft or mortar bomb. The link with the blonde female, however, is baffling.

ℬOTH BARRELS

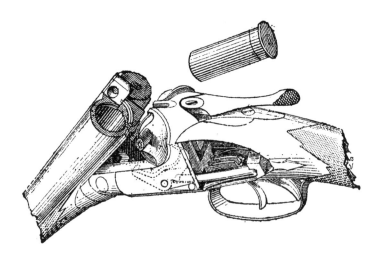

As in 'give them both barrels' or 'with both barrels' is to thoroughly chastise someone; when a horse kicks out with both rear legs simultaneously.

Shotguns, even during the muzzle-loading era, were generally *double-barrelled*. Firing *both barrels* together in quick succession delivered a devastating and deadly weight of fire.

ℬROADSIDE

To verbally overwhelm or intimidate someone.

A naval tactic employed when warships were armed with muzzle-loading cannons which fired from the sides of a ship. A *broadside* was the action of firing all available guns simultaneously on one side of a ship into an enemy vessel with deadly effect. This could only often be achieved after some very skilful seamanship and manoeuvring. The opportunity to deliver an effective broadside, because of the time scale and the fact that vessels were moving, was often limited, so timing was essential.

BULLETPROOF / BOMBPROOF

A highly exaggerated expression meaning the robustness of an object, plan, person or, indeed, animal; horses that are not phased or worried by traffic or disturbance are referred to as being 'bombproof'.

A derisive term used during the American Civil War to describe soldiers who went to great lengths to avoid action or exposure to enemy fire. Some senior officers were renowned for moving to the rear during a battle for the same reason. Infantry and artillery personnel would mouth the term to passing cavalry who they envied because of their ability to avoid harm through their mobility. The direct meaning, of course, describes sufficient physical protection from the direct threat of a bullet or explosion.

$\mathcal{B}$ULLSEYE

Hitting a target, finalising a deal. And trivially, for those who remember, a TV gameshow in the 1970s.

The origin of *bullseye* is rather unclear and there are a number of suggested connections with archery and firearms. The phrase *bull's eye* from the French, *oeil de boeuf* has been used in connection with many different things. There is a supposed connection with archery in medieval times when archers who were raised nationwide were expected to collectively practise their skills. This was often on Sundays after church services when communities met. The bleached white skull of a bull was, apparently, sometimes used as a target, and an arrow entering the eye orbit was simply termed as a *bull's eye hit*. There is the mention of a *bull's eye* as a target in 1833 in reference to firearms. It became commonplace in association with target shooting when the large targets used in archery practice were created with the centre of the target, so called the *bullseye*.

CALLING THE SHOTS

Someone obviously in charge, taking charge or heavily influencing a situation. As an aside, 'Call the shots' was a very successful single for the band Girls Aloud.

According to the OED, *calling the shots* would appear to be a recent phrase. It apparently first appeared in print in the late 1960s. An earlier phrase, *to call one's shots*, meaning to affirm your intention of achieving a goal before actually going after it, was in use by the 1930s. The origin of *call the shots* and *call one's shots* appears to stem from target shooting. In *calling one's shots* a target shooter announced in advance where on the target the shot was going to strike, which displayed his experience and skill. However, if someone else were *calling the shots*, the *shooter* would be playing to their tune, aiming and shooting where told.

In the days of pistol duelling the referee, having satisfied himself that both parties are squared up facing each other and ready, would, by a prearranged signal, call for their *shots to be fired*. This might have been a verbal command or something as simple as dropping a handkerchief.

In many ball game sports the direct associative references to *shooting* crop up frequently. The term manifests itself in the game of billiards or pool, wherein, at certain stages in the game, the player announces his proposed *shots* in advance.

CARTRIDGE

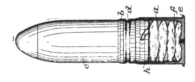

Associated with computer printers; a style of ink pen; a record player stylus.

A cylindrical tube, originally made of paper (see cartridge paper below), for containing a gunpowder charge and shot or bullet. Devised for military needs to aid load conformity, reloading speed, transportation and storage. Ultimately, developed into the self-contained, totally weatherproof metallic *cartridge* by the end of the 19th century.

51

CARTRIDGE PAPER

A high quality rough-textured paper.

Originally produced and used to fashion into tubes containing gunpowder and a bullet or shot with sealed ends for use in muzzle-loading weapons. The user would tear off the powder end with their teeth and then pour the charge into the barrel and push the rest of the cartridge with the projectile into the barrel and ram it down the breech with the ramrod. The outside of the cartridge was often smeared with some form of waterproofing grease, tallow, beeswax or animal fat. The waterproof smearing of military cartridges with grease from pig and beef fat was considered to be one of the contributing factors that sparked the Indian Mutiny in 1857.

Indian Sepoy troops, who formed part of the British Army abroad, were armed with muzzle-loading British Enfield rifles. These local troops discovered that the *paper cartridges* they were issued with were thus protected, but the pig fat was deeply repugnant to the Muslims in their ranks, as was, conversely, the cow sacred to the Hindus amongst them. Demonstrations started in February of 1857, but they were not handled at all well by the British military and authorities, and they failed to resolve the issue. The first violent revolt occurred at Meerut on May 10th where British troops were killed and so started a disastrous and bloody conflict in a turbulent part of the British Empire.

CAP GUN

Associated with toy guns that fire a roll of caps for sound effect.

Originally an actual ignition mechanism. This was developed in 1855 by an American dentist, Edward Maynard from Washington DC. In an attempt to spectacularly improve the tried and tested use of individual copper *percussion caps* that fired the muzzle-loading percussion military rifles of the time, Maynard created a device called a 'tape primer'. These were spaced and sealed dabs of priming compound on a roll of paper tape. This rolled tape was accommodated in a recess in front of the hammer with a hinged cover plate on the Model 1855 rifled musket.

When the firer cocked the weapon a pawl mechanism moved a fresh *cap* into place under the hammer, the idea being to eliminate the need for the firer to place individual caps on the action when preparing to fire. When the hammer struck and fired the weapon the spent cap was cut off. It was not a success in the field because it was simply not robust enough, and later models of the US Model 1855 were redesigned to use the standard copper cap.

CANNON FODDER

A rather derogatory term referring to persons surplus to requirement, of no importance or easily replaced.

Poor quality or conveniently positioned infantry sent in advance of a main attack to draw fire from the enemy's artillery, thus feeding the guns with *fodder* (horse feed) and keeping your adversary distracted and occupied.

Up until the later part of the nineteenth century warfare was generally fought very much in the open with masses of infantry and cavalry being pitched against each other. Attacks were often preceded with artillery, but the same attacks had to, in turn, face artillery. Troops in the open suffered heavy losses, but if it was considered necessary to distract an enemy, test their firepower or encourage them to expend ammunition then planned sacrifices were seen as acceptable.

Collins dictionary says it's a translation from German, *Kanonenfutter*. Former World War II veteren, lexographer and author of many a writing guide, Eric Partridge, writes in his *Word, Words, Words!* slang book '... *Kanonenfutter, cannon fodder, dates from long before the War; never very popular with British troops who, for the most part, found the joke too grim...*'

Caught in the crossfire

An uninvolved individual or a group inadvertently caught between two sides of a discussion, argument or debate and with no connection or allegiance to either side.

Innocent and uninvolved victims mistakenly occupying the ground between two sides engaged in a firefight or gun battle and suffering as a result. An enemy being successfully ambushed or engaged in a planned intersection of gunfire designed to maximise casualties and prevent escape.

CLAY PIGEON SHOOTING

A well-established popular shooting sport with many varying disciplines.

It is the first and only introduction to firearms and shooting for many people, and it is often included in outdoor corporate events. Whilst the term is not used outside the context, there are some interesting similes within the practise.

The mechanical devices used to dispense the clay targets are referred to as *traps* and the operator is referred to as a *trapper*. This is because the original targets were live pigeons, which were held in a cage trap, a door of which at the top could be opened by the trapper who pulled it open with a cord on command from the firer. Thus, we still use the term today and participants will be familiar with the term *pull* but might never have questioned its origin. The use of live birds was banned in the UK in 1921. Shooters will also refer to the clay targets as *birds* and a target that breaks as it leaves the trap is referred to as a *no bird*. A trap that dispenses a clay laterally, so that it rolls (and bounces) on its edge along the ground, is referred to as a *rabbit*. That can be more of a challenge than shooting a real live rabbit, actually. A successful hit might often be described and recorded on a score card as a *kill*.

The term *clay pigeon* has increasingly been superseded with the more politically correct and softer reference *clay target*, especially when included in corporate events.

COCKING A WEAPON

The mechanical action of preparing a firearm to fire. Later used to describe the preparation of a shutter on a traditional camera.

In the middle of the 16th century the snaphaunce firing mechanism was developed. This was really a modification of the wheel lock, and the forerunner of the flintlock.

There's apparently a German source for *snaphaunce* being *schnapphahn* 'snapcock'. This refers to the sharp and brisk forward and descending action of the lock on firing being a similar motion, especially when viewed in silhouette, to a cockerel pecking at food on the ground.

The flintlock is the perfected form of the snaphaunce. If the flash pan is open or must be uncovered by hand before firing the weapon it is a *snaphaunce*. If the flash pan cover is opened at the moment of firing, by the flint striking the sprung frizzen plate, then the weapon is a *flintlock*. The flintlock had many advantages; it could be carried with no danger of the priming powder falling out and it was better protected in wet conditions.

CROSSHAIRS /
IN THE CROSSHAIRS

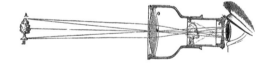

In the crosshairs; in the sights; a business acquisition may be referred to as such.

Telescopic weapon sights came into use during the 19th century and one of the earliest sighting arrangements set into the prism was a *crosshair*. The use of lenses created from polished rock crystal for magnification was well known in the ancient world. The Roman Emperor, Nero

(54–68AD), used a magnifying device called a *smaragdus*. The modern telescope is associated with Galileo Galilei (1564–1642).

The fine sighting crosshairs mounted into a rifle telescope are more correctly referred to as *graticules* or *reticules*. Prior to the attempted assassination of Democratic congresswoman Gabrielle Giffords in Tucson Arizona in January 2011, the outspoken US Republican Congresswoman Sarah Palin had rather unwisely posted a map of the USA on her website depicting gun sight crosshairs on areas of the country currently governed by her political rivals. It was an unfortunate example of imagery that might be forever linked to the tragedy.

CRUSADE / ON A CRUSADE

Somebody who is on a determined course of action, upholding a firmly held belief.

The origin is French *croisade*, which according to the OED literally means '*the state of being marked with a cross*' from the Latin *crux* 'cross'.

The grusome military campaigns called the *Crusades* of 1096–1291 were fuelled by a religious ideology of Christains and Muslims fighting over control of the Holy Lands. The Christian leaders of Rome in 11th century Europe where very powerful but wanted to never lose their control and influence over Europe and knew that tactically dominating the Holy Lands would secure their Christian authority.

There were a number of Crusades during this time including The People's Crusade, consisting of a too eager band of knights and common people who fell under the swords of the superior Turkish army. Soon after this failed attempt, scores of nights led The First Crusade (1096-1099) to the first very bloody Fall of Jerusalem, where many civilians lost their lives inspite of promises by the Crusaders to spare them. Following eight major Crusades the final major Crusades known as The Last Crusades, marked an end to the Crusaders and Crusader States with victory for the Muslim Mamluk soldiers after the fall of Tripoli in 1289, and the Seige of Acre in 1291.

Since the Crusades countless conflicts between Western governments and the Middle East have been refered to in the media on broadcasts and in print in terms of a *Crusade*.

ᴅEFUSE

To pacify, dampen down a situation;, to negotiate; to reach agreement without conflict.

Often confused with the term *diffuse*, the term is simple inasmuch as it describes the action of removing the *fuse* from an explosive device. An explosive device needs an initiator, which might be mechanical or electrical. This might be linked to a fuse, which is a timer set to manage the time from initiation to explosion. Modern devices can be very complex. IEDs used by terrorists can have additional initiators designed to override attempts to disarm them. They require highly skilled operators to *defuse* them. In the early days of simple explosives cutting or removing a burning fuse was often sufficient to stop an explosion.

$\mathcal{D}$IEHARD / $\mathcal{D}$IE HARD

The term is used to describe a person who stubbornly holds on to a minority view or opinion often in defiance of the circumstances or common sense. It rarely has anything to do with dying or exposing an individual to physical risk.

This term got a new lease of life when the action film *Die*

Hard was released in 1988, starring the actor, Bruce Willis. This was followed by three sequels *Die Hard 2* in 1990, *Die Hard With A Vengeance* in 1995, and *Live Free or Die Hard* in 2007.

The meaning of the term was apparently recorded in 1703 and it referred to a condemned man's approach to his forthcoming death. Executions carried out by hanging in London took place at Tyburn. The process meant that the victim was hauled up by the neck and thus died slowly of strangulation. Some chose to pay friends to hang onto their legs to quicken their deaths. Others were defiant and chose to involve audiences with their suffering and *die hard*. The trapdoor drop method of hanging that was designed to swiftly break the neck at the bottom of the drop was to come, in the future.

The term was renewed again following the Battle of Albuera of 1811 in Portugal during the Peninsular War. During the battle, an injured Lieutenant-Colonel William Inglis of the 57th (West Middlesex) Regiment, who had just been shot in the neck, stoically carried on and was reported to say '*Die hard men, die hard*' and '*Die hard fifty seventh!*' in encouragement during a renewed French attack. The West Middlesex's regiment appropriated the nickname *The Die Hards*. The term was later to be heard amongst the military hierarchy and political circles and described individuals who were resistant to change and proposed reform.

*D*OUBLE-EDGED SWORD

A plan, idea or action which may support the desired outcome because of its very robust construction with an answer for everything. Conversely it may be an action that could be turned on the initiator by an anticipating competitor.

Edged weapons were designed with blades, single-edged or *double-edged*. It was often purely down to design and preference. Some would argue that a double-edged weapon was of no advantage because you could only inflict a blow from one side anyway.

A stabbing weapon like a dagger or short sword might be double-edged, as might an edged projectile like a spear or arrowhead. A sabre was single-edged because it was primarily a cutting, slashing and bludgeoning weapon.

$\mathcal{D}$ODGING A BULLET

Somebody who is seemingly able to avoid or sidestep serious trouble, problems or accusations. It became a more commonly used idiom during the Coronavirus pandemic whereby people were describing themselves as having 'dodged a bullet' by avoiding a Covid-19 infection.

Persons in a firefight or facing an armed assault seemingly able to avoid being shot by virtue of their presence of mind, anticipation or speed of reaction reaching cover. Of course, it is impossible to *dodge a bullet* that might be travelling at between 1000-2500 feet per second, but it is possible to position oneself or select cover that will minimise the chance of being struck by one. *Dodging a bullet* in the literal sense is likely impossible and pure fantasy.

DON'T FIRE UNTIL YOU SEE THE WHITES OF THEIR EYES!

Do not act or commit until you are certain of success.

This command was attributed to William Prescott, an American officer, at the Battle of Bunker Hill on June 17th 1775, during the American War of Independence. Although the turn of phrase has also been linked to Major General Israel Putnam who was also at the battle at the time.

William Howe Downes writes in his article on 'Monuments and Statues of Boston' in *The New England Magazine* (September 1894 to February 1895): *'In Monument Square, Charlestown, near the base of the Bunker Hill Monument, stands the bronze heroic statue of Col. William Prescott, by W. W. Story. Prescott was one of the commanders of the American forces in the battle ... and he was the author of the immortal injunction, "Don't fire until I tell you ; don't fire until you see the whites of their eyes."'*

The common infantry weapon of the day was the smoothbore flintlock musket, which delivered a heavy lead ball three-quarter inch in diameter. It caused bone-shattering, gaping wounds and was effective against horses as well as men. The weapon was best utilised when it was fired in volleys by disciplined troops into the massed ranks of advancing enemy. Its disadvantage was inaccuracy, and an individual soldier was not expected to be able to hit a man-sized target beyond 75–100 yards with any degree of consistency.

Waiting until your enemy was well within effective range was the order of the day, unnerving though it must have been. In *An Essay on the Life of the Honourable Major General Israel Putnam* by Col. David Humphreys he writes: '*The lines advanced and soon opened to view. The American marksmen are with difficulty restrained from firing. General Putnam rode through the line, and ordered that no one should fire till they arrived within eight rods, nor any one till commanded. "Powder was scarce and must not be wasted. They should not fire at the enemy till they saw the white of their eyes, and then fire low, take aim at their waistbands. They were all marksmen, and could kill a squirrel at a hundred yards; reserve their fire, and the enemy were all destroyed. Aim at the handsome coats, pick off the commanders."'* He goes on to to say how the very same orders were heard and said by William Prescott and other officers at the battle, which all added to the mystery of who actually uttered the words first.

Other great leaders were also attributed with versions

of the order including Frederick the Great in the Battle of Prague in 1757, Prince Charles against the Austrian army at Jägendorf in 1745 and Lieutenant-Colonel Sir Andrew Agnew of Lochnaw, as instructions to the Royal Scots Fusiliers at the Battle of Dettingen in June 1743.

One cannot see the *whites of somebody's eyes* who is directly confronting you beyond 10-15 paces. This is an extremely short range to wait for. Perhaps this was always a gross exaggeration, but one can reason that the command was created to focus attention and discipline.

ᗩUEL

A physical, often sporting, challenge generally between two adversaries or friendly rivals.

Duelling became an excepted fatal practise to settle an argument, challenge, serious feud or disputed matter of honour between gentlemen. Associated with the privileged, but not always, it was conducted by them duelling, which became a very serious and coordinated practise that could result in the death of one of the challengers.

Jousting with lances on horseback was a form of duelling, but it is better remembered as a gentlemen's fight with swords or pistols. Firearms placed adversaries in a more even encounter; the young fit and nimble challenger armed with a sword might easily outmanoeuvre an aging and portly opponent, but armed with pistols it was a more even match. Gun makers specialised in making duelling pistols; these were exceptionally high quality, expensive firearms produced in boxed pairs. A *duel* was formally refereed and witnessed, and the adversaries were bound by strict rules. The last recorded pistol duel that took place in England occurred in 1850, but the practise continued in a clandestine fashion until it was recognised to be an illegal act.

The gunfight from American western myth was probably a far less disciplined affair with little evidence to prove that adversaries faced each other off, one beating the other to a draw in the middle of a dusty street. They were more likely to be messy drunken affairs with some people shot whilst unarmed or in the back whilst trying to run away.

Classic European duelling, whilst still a hideous undertaking, did encourage gentlemen to practise target shooting, and it was from this that the modern peaceful discipline of target pistol shooting emerged. The term *choose your weapons* can be linked to the serious days of duelling. Today we still use the term in a mocking and harmless fashion.

ℱACE THE MUSIC

Being prepared to face an uncomfortable or dreaded ultimatum, criticism or undertaking.

Some clear differences here; explanations include a soldier taking his place in the ranks during an assembly, so facing the military band; a cavalryman on parade trying to keep his restless horse quiet while a band is playing; or a soldier being drummed out of his regiment as a result of committing a crime or dishonourable behaviour. Some consider that it comes from musical theatre. A nervous or inexperienced performer would have to summon up all his or her courage to *face the audience*, which would also require them to *face the musicians* in a traditionally-positioned orchestra pit. These they fear might be a cynical and intolerant lot who won't support or suffer a fool.

𝓕IRING BLANKS

The sexual climatic endeavours of a man who has had a vasectomy.

The use of *blank* rounds in firearms training (military, police and shooting sports), military ceremonial (gun salutes), film or theatrical props, or as a scare charge (bird-scarers or sound mines). These detonate a propellant/explosive charge thus producing the sound effect but without firing a deadly projectile or creating blast. Military personnel make use of a large amount of *blank firing* ammunition for training and exercise purposes.

An attachment referred to as a *BFA* (Blank Firing Attachment) will often be seen attached to the muzzle of a weapon in this instance. It is usually coloured red or yellow. It is designed to confine sufficient expelled propellant gas to recycle a semi or fully automatic firing mechanism.

𝓕IREWORKS

The actual meaning is readily understood by most from an early age, but we still use the term to describe a scene, anticipated or otherwise. 'There's going to be fireworks', preceding a confrontation, for instance. We might also

mockingly refer to the traditional instruction to be found on a firework prior to goading a short-tempered person, 'Light blue touch paper and retire...'

The actual real date of the origination of *fireworks* is still unknown, but it is believed to have been invented by the Chinese about 2000 years ago. Author A. St. H. Brock in his seminal work *Pyrotechnics: The History and Art of Firework Making* published in 1918 writes: '*In India and China saltpetre (or nitrate of potash) is found in large quantities, and was, no doubt, used by the primitive inhabitants in far-off times for such purposes as curing meat, cooking, etc. The dropping of a quantity in the camp fire may have attracted the attention of some early inventor to the extent of starting him on a series of what were probably the earliest chemical experiments.*'

'*He would notice that the presence of saltpetre made the fire burn brighter, and its use as a tinder maker would suggest itself by mixing it with some substance which he knew to be combustible. The most common fuel he knew of was wood, but it must be a powder to mix evenly with saltpetre. Wood is not easily reduced to powder; saws had not been invented, so that he could not add sawdust, and the nearest thing he could get would be charcoal from the fire, which could easily be reduced to powder. With this mixture he would be well on the way to success in elementary pyrotechny.*'

73

The mixture burned well, and when compressed in an enclosure (a bamboo tube) the mixture exploded. Marco Polo is recorded to have seen fireworks in China between 1268 to 1273 and is linked with allegedly bringing the Chinese compound back to Europe in the 13th century, although some accounts suggest it was the Crusaders returning to Europe with the incredible *black powder*, also known as *gunpowder*. Once in Europe, this explosive mixture was experimented with for military purposes, first in crude rockets, then in cannons and guns. The English became particularly fascinated with fireworks for display purposes, and they became very popular during the reign of Queen Elizabeth I (1558–1603). She created the position of Fire Master of England.

In 1605, during the reign of King James I (1603–1625), Guy Fawkes and his fellow conspirators attempted to blow up the Parliament of Great Britain with 36 barrels of gunpowder in the cellars of Westminster Hall. Gunpowder was well developed as a weapon propellant and explosive by then. On the 5th November Fawkes and his fellow conspirators were caught and arrested, and Parliament was saved. That night is now celebrated as Bonfire Night with exploding fireworks and burning effigies of Guy Fawkes.

A delighted King James II (1685–1688) even knighted his Fire Master after seeing his spectacular coronation firework display.

ƑIRING LINE / ƖN THE FIRING LINE

'In the firing line' is a term used to describe people at the forefront of an operation, customer facing, at the mercy of customers and competitors.

A *firing line* was simply a held position over a manageable and effective front where troops discharged their weapons towards an advancing enemy. More relevant in the days of muzzle-loading and single-shot weapons where the control and weight of fire was more critical. The *firing line* faced the enemy and, as such, troops in this forward position were also exposed to fire coming from the enemy. *Out of the firing line* was naturally a safer position and a haven, sometimes unfairly, sought and regularly occupied by some.

𝓕IRST-RATE

This very innocuous term is a means of describing a value or perceived value of a commodity or person in any context. Used also in conjunction with the terms 'second-rate' or 'third-rate', meaning exactly as the terms would imply— inferior or not up to top specification.

The designation of warships in the Royal Navy saw complex and major changes from the beginning of the 17th century and these changes continued to be revised into the 19th century. Warships in the reign of Charles I had been ranked, but later they would be *rated*. Samuel Pepys, the famous diarist and a very astute administrator, when he was Secretary to the Admiralty, revised the structure in 1677. The *rating* of a ship was assigned to quantify administrative requirements and military use.

The number and weight of guns determined the size of crew needed and hence the amount of ammunition, stores, pay and rations required. The trend was for each rating to have a greater number of guns and subsequent gun decks to accommodate them. There were a number of revisions over time, but Pepys set a *first-rate* ship to have 90–100 guns, then by 1801, 100–120 guns. A second-rate ship by the start of the 18th century mounted 90 to 98 guns on three-gun decks. There was a significant overhaul in February 1817 where the first-rates from that date included all of the three-deckers, the new second-rate, the two-deckers of 80 guns or more, and the third-rate was reduced to two-deckers with less than 80 guns. Ship rating even went as far as sixth-rate.

The term *second-rate* has since passed into our language as an adjective used to define quality inferior to *first-rate*. This means of reference and comparison was never relevant to naval classification; the terms have simply been corrupted. In the Royal Navy today, junior ranks are still referred to as *Ratings*.

ℱLAGSHIP

The deemed leader or leading commodity or a representative location. A leading restaurant might be deemed the 'flagship' of a restaurant consortium or empire.

A naval vessel carrying a senior naval officer, usually of the rank of Admiral. In a fleet of warships the *flagship* is the leading platform for an operation. It is from here that senior staff will plan and implement an operation or fight a battle. Admiral Horatio Nelson was aboard his flagship HMS Victory at the battle of Trafalgar in 1805. The ship was commanded by Captain Thomas Hardy. Nelson was killed by a French sniper, a musket ball initially entering his shoulder and lodging in his spine.

𝓕LAK / 𝓣AKE THE FLAK

To offer or be subjected to criticism or ridicule.

Derived from the German ground fire ordinance directed at military aircraft during the Second World War; from the German *Fliegerabwehrkanone* 'aviator-defence gun'. Now generally referred to as *triple A* (Anti-Aircraft Artillery). Prior to the term *flak*, anti-aircraft fire was described as *Ack-Ack*, which was the military signaller's phonetic reference for the letters *AA* (Anti-Aircraft). Phonetic for the letter *A* is now *Alpha*.

ℱLASH IN THE PAN

An anticipated event, plan or happening that is short-lived, disappoints or eventually comes to nothing.

The gunpowder in the *flash pan* on a flintlock weapon being initiated by the sparks generated on the frizzen plate but failing to ignite the main charge and ultimately firing the weapon. A misfire such as this was generally caused by a blockage in the touchhole or vent that led to the main charge in the barrel chamber.

An alternative describes it as being the disappointing discovery of iron pyrites (fool's gold), rather than real gold flecks *flashing*, amongst the stone, mud, water and debris in the gold prospector's pan.

The firer in this image has pulled the trigger of this reproduction 18th century musketoon and it shows the flint held in the jaws of the lock striking the frizzen plate and creating a flash of sparks. The frizzen plate has sprung forward exposing the gunpowder in the pan which is igniting. A split second later the flash reached the main charge in the barrel chamber via the touchhole which ultimately discharged the weapon. If it had failed as a result of bad loading or a blocked vent only the small amount of gunpowder held in the pan would have ignited, hence the phrase *flash in the pan*.

FREEZE THE BALLS OFF A BRASS MONKEY

A very old English expression for defining very cold weather.

A fanciful adaptation but apparently untrue is that *cannon balls* on board warships were neatly piled into pyramids inside a *brass monkey*, a low brass ring which kept them in place. If it became cold enough for the monkey ring to contract, this would supposedly upset the pile and cause them to move or roll.

Naval ammunition was actually stored in shot garlands, wooden plinths with holes cut in rows sufficient to accommodate cannon balls and stop them from rolling about a ship at sea. The term does not apparently have a truly understood origin, but the old favourite just proves how we enjoy a good story.

FRONTLINE

In the forefront; in business to symbolise a lead corporate position or organisational stance fronting challenges with practised and developed responses.

A position description of military forces in direct contact with an enemy. The frontal arrangement and dispositions of an army or a subunit in defence or in preparation for an attack. Historically, the most exposed and dangerous location. Modern warfare and weapon delivery, however, can expose all elements, even those in the rear and not in direct contact.

*F*USILLADE

A sustained or overwhelming outburst of criticism.

The *fusil* was a French reference for a flintlock musket and this weapon was best utilised when it was volley-fired by massed troops, thus the *fusillade*. The flintlock ignition system was recorded in use in the later 17th century. It was vastly more efficient and superior to the standard and established matchlock which required the firer to keep a matchcord alight in order to fire it.

Fusiliers, already incorporated into some continental armies, were also raised within the British Army to be trained in the use of this new system, and they were initially tasked to escort artillery units. Horse-drawn artillery batteries were required to transport large quantities of gunpowder for their cannons, and when they came into action large quantities were exposed in opened containers. Matchlock firearms with their smouldering matchcords were obviously dangerous in this vicinity, and so the task went to the specially trained Fusiliers with their new 'modern' weapons; attention to health and safety is nothing new. The Royal Regiment of Fusiliers still exists today.

𝓕USE / SHORT FUSE

This term is used in a vast array of metaphors and idioms.

In this instance it is meant to associate with the initiator of an explosive device rather than the electrical application. The phrase 'short fuse' describes a person with a short temper or a low threshold for remaining calm in a stressful situation. Lighting someone's fuse is the act of intentionally or otherwise provoking a short-tempered person.

A *fuse* linked to an explosive is simply an initiator allowing the operative to withdraw from the scene or throw a grenade or deliver fired ordnance into a proposed killing ground before it explodes.

In the 16th and 17th century, troops called grenadiers were trained to throw grenades in battle, which was a precarious task lighting the fuse and the timing of throwing the grenade. Early fuses were simply cords soaked in a flammable compound which burnt down to the main body of the explosive and detonated it. The length of the fuse determined the time delay. Fusing systems on modern weapons are of course far more sophisticated.

During the Falklands war, Argentinean warplanes attacking the British forces bridgehead in Falkland Sound were delivering bombs that were fused incorrectly. Releasing them from very low altitude against ships, the weapons were not fully arming and despite accurately striking targets a proportion passed through superstructure and decks causing extensive damage and casualties but not exploding.

GOING POSTAL

Descending into a rage; someone becoming significantly upset and resorting to angry and, perhaps, abusive outbursts.

This is very much an Americanism and means the same as *going ballistic* (see **Ballistic / Going ballistic** on page 28). It relates back to a series of mass shooting incidents in the USA between 1970 and 2003 that took place in US Postal facilities when disgruntled employees turned on fellow staff and management. It would not be accurate and, indeed, entirely unfair to suggest that the US Postal Service provoked such behaviour; it is more likely the irony associated with these occurrences in official Federal premises. Research supported by the US National Institute of Justice shows mass shootings in the USA occur mostly in the workplace, and secondly, in retail locations.

Going over the top

Somebody exaggerating a requirement or action; going beyond acceptable limits. A fanciful way of announcing the initiation of a challenging action, task or activity.

Now even abbreviated to the term *OTT*. Originates from the often highly dangerous and almost suicidal action during the 'Great War' of leaving the safety of a trench and advancing towards an enemy still in a defensive position and thus being exposed and having little protection from directed fire. Reference to the term appeared in a publication of *War Illustrated* in 1916.

Gun to the head / Holding a gun to the head

A verbal threat; an intimidation tactic; an ultimatum directed towards an individual or a group, usually associated with unfair and unscrupulous behaviour.

Holding a *gun* towards somebody's *head* is the ultimate in violent threatening behaviour and could be associated with someone wanting control in a desperate situation, perhaps at the scene of an armed robbery or hostage taking.

Hair trigger

Somebody who has a short-tempered disposition or is easily riled or excited.

A firearm *trigger* that has been adjusted to release the sear with a minimum of finger pressure as an aid to minimise weapon movement to optimise maximum accuracy. Specialist firearms, target rifles and pistols, duelling pistols and sniper rifles might have adjustable triggers meaning that the pressure to release a shot can be mechanically adjusted.

HANG FIRE

Slow to act; a stalled result or outcome whereupon interested parties await an outcome.

An extended pause between the flash pan charge in a flintlock igniting the main charge or a detonated cap on a percussion firearm being heard briefly before the main charge igniting. This was largely eradicated with the introduction of self-contained cartridges, because of the close and sealed positioning of the detonating cap and the main charge.

HEADHUNTER / HEADHUNTED / HEADHUNTING

An executive personnel recruiter whose job is to search and find suitable, and often very valuable, staff to fill positions within organisations or corporations.

The origin of this is more literal: According to OED '*a member of a people that collects the heads of the people they kill*'.

The Dyaks of Borneo are the most noted *headhunters*. The term has also been associated with people who were prepared to travel the world at great expense to shoot big game and procure decorative trophies.

HUNG, DRAWN AND QUARTERED

When someone is severely berated or criticised.

It might just be possible that the infrequency that this term is now used in conversation might have something to do with a greater understanding of what it means. This particularly gruesome form of execution was in practise before the use of firearms but is worthy of mention. This was a capital punishment reserved for the worst crimes, namely treason.

After being sentenced, malefactors were usually imprisoned, sometimes for days, then dragged (*drawn*) by a horse to the place of execution, usually tied on a hurdle, which is a wheelless, uncomfortable wooden frame. Once stripped of their clothing, they were taken to the gallows scaffold and *hanged*, but only to cause strangulation and near-death. They were then disembowelled and those still able to witness life might have had the further misfortune of having their guts burnt. The head was removed and then cut into four (*quartered*). The four parts of the body were then displayed publicly, perhaps as a warning to others, although hangings attracted big crowds and some believed the body parts to be magical; onlookers often stole or fought over others to touch the corpses.

The first recorded instance of a person being *hanged, drawn and quartered* in England is that of William Maurice, who in 1241 was convicted of piracy. The Scottish knight William Wallace was also put to death in this manner, captured and tried in 1305, and executed in London. His severed head was placed on a spike on London Bridge while his arms and legs were displayed at various towns across England and Scotland. For his part in the Gunpowder Plot on November 5th 1605, Guy Fawkes, along with eight surviving conspirators, was hanged, drawn and quartered between 30-31 January 1606. This came as a result of a failed attempt to kill James I and replace him with a Catholic monarch. But, to avoid the horror and pain of disembowelment, Guy Fawkes jumped from the scaffold before the noose was tight and broke his neck. However, he didn't escape disembowelment and quartering.

Some historical factual disputes remain over the wording sequence of *hanged, drawn and quartered*, and also to the definition of *drawn*; some historians assert that *drawn* was something done *after hanging* and meant it as the removal of the intestines, such as you would prepare a chicken for roasting. But the action of *draw or drawn or drawing* is defined by the OED as '*pull or drag ... so as to make it follow behind*', and it is clear this was done *before* the hanging, which is certainly recorded in various publications including *Reeves' History of the English Law* published in the 19th Century by W. F. Finlason '... *the judgment of high treason was pronounced as follows: that he should be carried back to the Tower of London, should be put on a hurdle, and drawn through the middle of the city to Tyburn, and there hanged by the neck; before he was dead his heart should be cut out, his head cut off, and his body divided into four parts, to be at the disposal of the king...*'

Perhaps we've confused ourselves over time in that respect.

*I*N THE LINE OF FIRE

A person subjecting themselves to threat, or having to be responsible for the result of a threat, a danger or a badly conducted plan.

Technically, according to *Instruction Upon the Art of Pointing Cannon, For The Use of Young Sea Officers* written in 1848, '*The vertical plane which passes through the axis of the bore of a gun is called the line of fire.*' A person *in the line of fire* in military terms was occupying a space in the ranks that was delivering fire to an enemy. This in turn might also have been a position that was exposed to receiving enemy small arms or artillery fire. Such persons were true combatants as opposed to those in the rear and away from action who were *out of the line of fire.*

𝓘NCENDIARY

A tendency towards very strong beliefs or feelings; inciting argument and sedition.

An *incendiary* device is an explosive designed to create fire. The petrol bomb or Molotov cocktail is a simple incendiary device. It is merely a glass bottle full of petrol with a flammable piece of material plugging the neck. This is lit and once the glass smashes it bursts into a small firebomb. More sophisticated weapons have been developed such as napalm and white phosphorus, both now banned.

*I*ncoming

Shouted or remarked as a warning at the first sign of an anticipated person entering a room or a situation, or message manifesting itself that will affect a group. May be used as a derogatory remark or, conversely, as a gesture of affection.

A verbalised warning confirming the arrival of enemy fire, artillery shells, airborne munitions, bombs, etc.

*I*N YOUR SIGHTS

Referring to an objective, or a person in some instances, for personal gain, reward or satisfying desire.

Reference to a target being focused on through a weapon *sight*. A traditional open sight arrangement (not being a telescopic sight) consisted of an adjustable backsight and a foresight. These were lined up with the intended target using one open eye; the right, for a right-handed shooter.

𝒥UMP THE GUN

A person's action or response that is too far in advance to be wholly effective; an ill-timed action, forward of an ideal; a badly anticipated start.

An athlete or adventurer attempting to gain advantage or over-anticipating the start of a race in advance of a starter's pistol shot. Ironically, many sporting events traditionally started with the official starter's blank-firing pistol have now opted for the protracted, sterile sound of a klaxon. This is because in modern times the sight of a starter using a blank-firing firearm at a sporting event has been deemed politically incorrect.

President Benjamin Harrison authorised the Oklahoma Territory Land Rush in 1889. The first Oklahoma Land Rush occurred on April 22nd 1889. The start was marked by the firing of a small cannon whereupon fifty to sixty thousand people raced into the Oklahoma Territory to plant personal stake flags on proposed town lots and farm claims. Those who had slipped past army guards who had been officially securing the start line were dubbed as *sooners* and were said to have *jumped the gun*.

KEEPING YOUR POWDER DRY

Exercising caution or keeping a low profile.

Referring to soldiers taking great care to keep their personal stocks of black *gunpowder dry* in wet weather. Damp gunpowder is useless and so it needed to be protected. Artillery probably had greater problems because they had to protect large quantities of gunpowder for their cannons. Infantry soldiers were issued with stocks of gunpowder which was initially held in a powder flask. This had a measuring device through which it was poured to charge a gun. When powder charges were later made up into cartridge paper (see **Cartridge paper** on page 52) some effort was made to protect them from damp and wet by coating them in animal fat or grease. Oliver Cromwell was documented to have urged his troops about to cross a river: '*Put your trust in God, my boys, and keep your powder dry.*'

𝒦EEP YOUR HEAD DOWN / 𝒦EEPING YOUR HEAD DOWN

Remaining out of sight or unnoticed, especially during a demanding period.

A simple term reminding combatants or involved victims

to stay behind cover from enemy fire and not to expose themselves to danger. When explosives detonate or bullets are fired the forces they generate and harness do most damage in unobstructed space. Being close to the ground, below ground or behind cover will help to minimise the chance of being struck.

LIMBER UP / LIMBERING UP

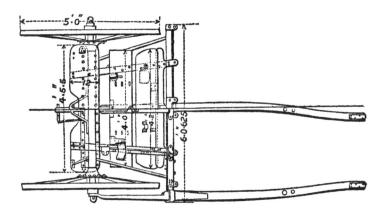

A term used to instruct military personnel or athletes to warm up before a physical activity. It could certainly be considered relevant to that end, especially as the very term refers to limbs i.e. arms and legs.

Also linked to *limber* are the terms *nearside* and *offside*, terminology we still use today to describe *left* and *right*. But where does it originate from?

The limber was a two-wheeled vehicle devised when artillery pieces were placed on two-wheeled carriages and became mobile. The limber was a simple cart with a pintle tow hook to which was attached the gun or piece for transit. Horses were harnessed in pairs either side of a limber pole that extended from the front of the limber. Six horses were preferred, but four was the considered minimum. The gun crew had to be accommodated and, with only room for two or three on the limber, a crew rider straddled each of the left hand *near* horses and held reins for both the horse he rode and the horse to his right, which was referred to as the *off* horse.

Ammunition was carried and distributed on the limber in ammunition chests or in another cart called a *caisson*. The whole arrangement was a large articulating vehicle. When the artillery piece was in action, the limber and caisson were a minimum of six yards behind the piece. The American Civil War saw the use of artillery on a grand scale and tactics and equipment were procured and directly copied from European armies.

When a gun was being brought out of action and preparation was being made to move, among many of the words of command were the orders '*Limber up!*' and '*Limber the guns!*'

ᴸOADED FOR BEAR

Well prepared; anticipating trouble; taking steps to protect oneself.

The action of choosing a suitable firearm and ammunition for protection in the wild. In the days of muzzle-loaders that might have entailed carrying and being prepared to fire the heaviest *loads* available. Muzzle-loaded weapons not firing a self-contained cartridge could be audaciously *loaded*, depending on the game being pursued or from what the firer was defending himself against. In locations where he feels thus threatened, he may choose to load his piece with a maximum powder and bullet charge to give himself the best chance of survival if threatened or attacked. A wild bear is a large animal and determined if angered. Even wounding one wouldn't prevent it from continuing an attack, so maximum firepower was essential.

𝓛OCK, STOCK AND BARREL

All the parts and features of an object, situation or property.

All the main parts that make up the separate components of a firearm. The *lock* no longer exists on a modern firearm in the manner it did up to the later part of the 19th century. The lock is now an internal feature that combines the mechanical features that load the weapon, fire it and carry out any ejection process. The *stock* is the wooden or plastic feature of a rifle or shotgun that the firer uses to support the weapon with the butt fitting into the shoulder. The *barrel*? Well, that hasn't changed a bit.

*L*OCK 'N' LOAD

Very much a military Americanism; an announcement for the preparation for something or a term to encourage an action. It is a term that most Americans would understand the true meaning of simply because as a nation they have a wider understanding about firearms.

This derives directly from military weapon-handling instructions. It describes the action of *locking* (attaching) a magazine or depressing a clip of ammunition into a weapon and then *loading* the first round into the chamber by working the action appropriate to the weapon to achieve it.

British military instruction drills achieve the same, but the wording is different. '*Load!*' is the instruction to attach a full magazine, depress a clip or place a belt of ammunition into the action. This is followed by the term '*Make Ready!*' or '*Ready!*', which is the instruction to operate the cocking handle or bolt to feed a round into the chamber ready for firing. I first came across the American term in

1980 when working with the United States Marine Corps (USMC) out of Camp Lejeune in South Carolina. On exercise (using blank ammunition), and under the command of an enthusiastic young USMC Lieutenant, we first received the command as we moved out of a patrol base.

*L*OOPHOLE

A mistake or piece of vague wording (sometimes in law) that allows someone to avoid prosecution, or to avoid obeying a law or instruction, or keeping to an agreement or contract. This might also be to the disadvantage of others or indeed compound a danger or threat to others.

Loopholes (also known as *balistraria*) were vertical and horizontal slits cut into the walls of castles and solid fortifications allowing defenders to fire arrows or firearms at an assaulting enemy while remaining protected. They were constructed in such a way as to allow the defender to fire oblique (diagonally) to the opening, which gave them more protection against returning fire; they were initially more commonly referred to as *arrow-loops*. To use a loophole, where you could direct fire at an exposed enemy outside a fortification, was an obvious advantage. Similarly, murder holes were openings built into the roof section between the main gate and an inner portcullis of a fortification where arrows, rocks and hot liquids could be dropped onto an enemy below.

*L*OOSE CANNON

An unreliable or untrustworthy person who is liable to upset or cause problems.

Naval deck artillery in the days of square riggers and muzzle-loading guns ran on wheeled carriages, so they could be manually hauled on board by gun crews to be loaded and then ran out, such that the muzzle protruded through a gun port for firing. They were hauled, manoeuvred and secured by ropes. If a gun (that could typically weigh over a ton) became insecure, especially in rough weather, it would create a very dangerous situation and potentially cause a lot of damage and inconvenience.

Magazine

An illustrated periodical, extended newspaper, or a specific-interest regular publication.

A lightweight, metal, spring-loaded detachable box that contains rifle or pistol rounds that is attached to a firearm. A *magazine* is also a storage space for military munitions. On warships these are often below the waterline and in the most protected part of a ship. According to OED, various origins including from the Arabic, *makzin, makzan* 'storehouse'.

ℳAGNUM

To mean bigger and better. Trivially, an ice cream brand owned by the Anglo-Dutch Unilever company.

As with wine and works of musical prowess, its meaning is relative. In the late 18th century *magnum* was first used as an expression or name to describe extra-large bottles of wine, and *magnum opus* was used to denote a composer's best work. Magnum doesn't necessarily mean *biggest* and *best*; it merely infers it.

The reference *magnum* has long had mythical connotations when it comes to guns and ammunition. Possibly the earliest use of the term came in the latter half of the 1800s, when the British applied it to particularly large cartridges such as the 500/450 Magnum Express. Supposedly, comparison of these large cartridge cases with previous smaller cases brought to mind the difference between standard and magnum-sized wine bottles. Whatever the origin, the term has endured. The Magnum .44 (forty-four) revolver was made famous by way of the Harry Callahan

(Clint Eastwood) *Dirty Harry* films; Callahan carried the long-barrelled weapon that, as he described, could '*Blow your head clean off.*'

MINEFIELD

A host of problems, obstacles or bureaucratic barriers that might stand in the way of a plan, purchase, claim or proposal.

A very exaggerated term when one considers the true meaning and purpose of a *minefield*. That being an area of land or sea denied to an enemy by virtue of concealed, placed explosives deployed to kill or maim personnel on foot or in vehicles or ships, triggered by pressure, movement, interference or remote initiation. Determined advance through such dangerous areas demands highly specialised detection, route marking and disarmament skills. Mine-fields should, rather paradoxically, be clearly marked and accurately recorded in order to protect friendly forces as well as intimidate enemies.

There are numerous badly marked and unmarked mine-fields in war-torn regions of the world that continue to threaten the very brave specialists who are employed to clear them. Mines and IEDs (Improvised Explosive Devices) continue to kill and injure non-combatants, livestock, and domestic and wild animals many years after a conflict. Princess Diana championed the Ottawa Treaty in 1997, which focused on the huge problems associated with global mine clearance.

MISFIRE

A plan, approach or objective that has failed. Also, an

irregular firing sequence in an internal combustion engine.

In the early days of firearms the methods of ignition were very rudimentary. The matchlock system had a burning cord that came into contact with a small pan of gunpowder sighted alongside a touchhole, which then led to the main charge in the barrel chamber. A blockage in the vent, rain or damp, or a failure to ignite the process was a simple *misfire*.

As systems became more sophisticated, wheel lock, snaphaunce and flintlock reliability improved, but misfires could still occur for the same reasons. Further development over the years with ignition systems, the evolving technology of the percussion cap, and then self-contained metallic cartridges, minimised misfires even further. Fortunately, modern weapons today rarely misfire, and if they do it is generally the mechanics that ultimately drives the firing pin into the cap on the base of a cartridge that can fail, rather than the cartridge itself.

There was a drill associated with the Swedish Carl-Gustav 84mm anti-tank weapon, which was a shoulder-fired anti-armour weapon in use with the British forces between 1968–1997. If the weapon failed to fire after two attempts, the firer instructed the No 2 (loader) '*Misfire unload!*' The weapon was unloaded, the failed round was ejected and another, loaded into place.

$\mathcal{N}$O QUARTER GIVEN

Offering or displaying no mercy to an opponent or competitor.

No quarter given, or *no quarter was given*, according to Penguin Dictionary of English Idioms literally means *'no mercy was shown, no man's life was spared.'* The term originates from an order by the commander of a victorious army that they *will not quarter* (shelter or accommodate) captured enemy soldiers. Therefore, none can be taken prisoner and all enemy combatants must be killed. Under the laws of war it is now especially forbidden to declare that *'no quarter will be given'*. This was established under Article

23 of *Convention (IV) respecting the Laws and Customs of War on Land and its annex: Regulations concerning the Laws and Customs of War on Land. The Hague, 18 October 1907.*

OPEN SEASON

More of an Americanism, meaning no restrictions or a free for all. Used in all contexts from personal associations to business.

Certain wildlife are protected from shooting and hunting around the world, and circumstances and rules vary dramatically. Certain game may be hunted and shot at particular times in the year. The pheasant season in the UK, for instance, runs from 1st October to 1st February of each year. *Open season* (in season) therefore describes an open or legitimate period. Vermin and some dangerous predators may be shot at any time; their demise is not restricted to a particular season.

ON TARGET

Achieving an objective or fulfilling a requirement within a time frame.

Shots delivered from small arms or artillery which are accurately hitting the desired target, be they ranged features, objects or persons.

OVER THE HUMP

Getting over the most difficult phase of a project, plan or operation in any context from a war to planning a party; the worst is over or over the worst.

During the Second World War USAAF and RAF transport aircraft crews were flying supplies from India to allied Chinese bases. Their routes east, to avoid Japanese interception, took them over some very inhospitable regions with weather systems influenced by the Himalayas, which was the most demanding duration period of their missions—navigation, cold, oxygen supply and the isolation. It was a relief to have got *over the hump*.

PARTING SHOT / PARTHIAN SHOT

A concluding remark; a closing gesture or even just a glance reserved for the moment of departure.

Actually, before the invention of firearms this was a military tactic developed by *Parthian* horsemen from the ancient Asian kingdom in what is now North-East Iran. They would feign a withdrawal or retreat and draw their pursuing enemies into a killing zone whereupon they would turn about at a predetermined point and, quite unexpectedly, fire deadly volleys of arrows back towards their surprised enemies.

In the year 53 BC Marco Casio invaded Parthia with an army of 40,000 men to continue expansion of the Roman Empire. He was unsuccessful and this was in part due to the design of the Parthian bow, a weapon made with a laminated spring, with a superior range and power that was more difficult for the Romans to defend against. 20,000 Romans died and 10,000 were taken prisoner.

$\mathcal{P}$OINT-BLANK / $\mathcal{P}$OINT-BLANK RANGE

Close proximity; in no uncertain terms; a face-to-face, abrupt declaration or announcement with no room for discussion.

Apparantly, 16th century in origin from the words *point* (pointing a weapon at a target) and *blank* (white), effectively meaning *hitting a white spot in the centre of a target*. In order to hit the white spot at *point-blank range*, you would have to be close enough that when you fired a projectile it would travel horizontally without dipping (it's trajectory going in a downwards direction) and hit the target.

These words written in 1848 taken from *Instruction Upon the Art of Pointing Cannon, For The Use of Young Sea Officers* helps explain: *'The motion of the bullet is then modified at each instant, by the resistance of the atmosphere, and by gravitation. This last force tends incessantly to draw it down until it finishes its flight by encountering the earth. The curve line which the centre of gravity of the ball describes in this flight, is called the trajectory.'*

In simple terms *point-blank range* describes the optimum distance a projectile, perhaps a bullet or cannon shell, has to travel to hit a target without deviation from its horizontal path. In the days of muzzle-loading cannons these big guns had a larger diameter at the breech (base) than the muzzle (firing end), so when they were aimed the bore would not be completely parallel to the line of sight to the target; in fact, it would be raised up. Knowing this, plus factoring in the charge to be used and weight of ammunition and effects of recoil, involved a calculation to either lower or raise the cannon in order to achieve point-blank range, hence this statement in the above source mentioned: *'The name of point blank range is given to the range obtained when the line of metal is horizontal.'*

However, *point-blank range* has commonly been associated with *extreme close range*. In forensics, gunshot wounds on flesh from *point-blank* are often identified by extensive powder burns and tissue damage from perforation by unburned grains of propellant.

𝒫ULLING THE PIN

Initiating an argument or provocation; intentionally creating tension and discontent.

The action of extracting the safety *pin* from a hand grenade prior to throwing it allows the sprung safety lever mechanism to initiate the fuse and a timed detonation process to take place. Grenade pins are held firmly in place and require a concerted force to remove them. Using your teeth, Hollywood-style, is not recommended.

℘UTTING YOUR HEAD ABOVE THE PARAPET

Somebody exposing themselves to criticism, unwanted attention, or a willingness to risk their reputation or security.

Very much a macho business term but nowhere near the true origin of the physical risk that referred to soldiers *looking over a trench parapet* to observe their enemy at the risk of attracting deadly sniper fire. Although the use of trenches can be traced back to the Crimean War and American Civil War, it was the stalemate of the trench warfare in Europe during the First World War that supposedly gave rise to this term. Troops devised all sorts of methods to enable them to see safely over their trench parapets, armoured observation positions and periscopes among them.

QUICK ON THE DRAW / QUICK ON THE TRIGGER

Fast, opportunistic, decisive.

American Western myth had gunslingers wearing low-slung gun belts with greased holsters. The action of bringing a pistol out of the holster to fire it was termed simply as *drawing*, ultimately to achieve the *fast draw* and first kill. In reality, handguns were not carried in low-slung holsters, but rather on the waist or in a pocket. Experienced gunman and law officers maintained that a steady nerve and the ability to shoot accurately were the most relevant skills and were far more important than outright speed. It would seem that Hollywood has made a good job of building on the myth, creating poetic licence and building up the legendary gun fight.

The tragedy that took place in Tucson Arizona on the 8th January 2011 where a crazed gunman shot US Representative Gabby Giffords as well as 18 others, which resulted in the deaths of 6 people, brought attention to the metaphor-laden, gun-toting coarseness of American politics. Some felt this outrage came as a result of this highly charged rhetoric. The state of Arizona has a colourful history, and the region is still very much associated with the gun-and-holster justice and culture of the 'Old West'.

RAMROD STRAIGHT

A physically erect person with good posture.

Muzzle-loading small arms required a *ramrod* that was often secured in a tube under the barrel of a personal weapon. Artillery pieces and naval muzzle-loading cannons also required the same apparatus, but it was generally

121

referred to as a *rammer*. It was a very strong and *straight rod* often made of hickory or steel. *Ramrods* are still used for attaching accoutrements for cleaning the barrels of modern firearms.

$\mathcal{R}$ICOCHET

A deflected shot in ball sports, which actually is representative of the behaviour of a fired projectile.

A bullet or projectile striking a flat surface at an oblique angle (an angle neigher at right angles nor parallel) can produce the phenomenon. Such a projectile is still hazardous and continues to carry energy. This word is not often used in many contexts directly away from its actual ballistic meaning, but it can be used to describe someone's action or a behavioural response. It is believed to have an origin in French, but the early construction and establishment of the word is obscure.

RECOIL

The action of stepping back in shock as a result of a statement or action.

Science reminds us that with every action there is a reaction. When a firearm is discharged the projectile is propelled forwards, but a rearward force, the *recoil*, is felt by the firer. The amount depends on the size and weight of the firearm and the charge it fires. Also referred to as *kick*, it can be unpleasant for an inexperienced or overly timid firer, or after having to fire off a lot of ammunition. The .45 Martini-Henry single-shot military rifle of the 1870s was well known for its heavy recoil.

ℛEVOLVER

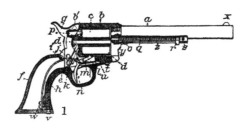

The term was used as a title for a Beatles record album written and recorded in the mid 1960s, supposedly describing the revolving action of a record on a turntable.

Apart from that one deviation, which was never meant to refer to a firearm, the noun is only used to describe a handgun, the mechanism of which being originally perfected and made famous by Samuel Colt from the early 19th century. Ironically, John Lennon would be shot and killed outside his home in the Dakota building in New York by a deranged fan, Mark David Chapman, in December 1980. Chapman used a .38 *revolver*.

ℛIDING SHOTGUN

Occupying the front passenger seat next to the driver in a vehicle. It might have a practical benefit as an aid to navigate or give directions, for instance, but in general terms it might be sought as the most comfortable position in what might be a vehicle full of passengers.

A term derived from the 19th century American West when a stagecoach or horse-drawn vehicle was being driven through potentially hostile regions. An armed passenger or associate accompanied the driver and would often choose a *shotgun*, because it was easy to load and fire a shot charge, which was deadly at close range. There was also more chance of hitting an attacker whilst taking aim on board a lurching and pitching vehicle. The driver would sit on the right because the brake was on this side and the *shotgun* would be on the left, which suited the vast majority who were right-handed, thus the weapon was pointing left. Wells Fargo, the famous US stagecoach line, armed their guards with large-calibre 10-gauge shotguns.

Riding shotgun in a left-hand drive vehicle, therefore, doesn't adhere to historical practice.

ℛIFLE

This generalised term for a shoulder-fired firearm deserves more than just a simple reference. Connected through the same root is the term we use to describe the action of searching in a hurried fashion.

The term *rifle* comes from French/Germanic origin *rifler* 'grooved or scratched'. Firearm exponents pondered on how they could improve the range and accuracy of early firearms. They already knew that the spin imparted on an arrow or crossbow bolt by feathered flights improved these requirements. The idea of cutting spiralling grooves inside a weapon barrel to enable spin on a tight-fitting bullet (which produced a better gas seal) came as a result. This was also extended to handguns and artillery. Quite who invented rifling is unknown; the data that did exist is lost, but it is considered that the idea proliferated in Germany or Austria.

Early rifles began being used towards the end of the 15th century, but it wasn't until the early 19th century that they became more widespread and accepted. The British Army had been impressed by the American militia they faced during the American War of Independence in 1776 who, armed with small calibre flintlock rifles, had caused much harm amongst the traditional open deployment of troops wearing colourful uniforms. They had also been studying elements of the Prussian forces and their use of Jaeger riflemen employing similar tactics.

The Army adopted the Baker rifle in 1807. This was a flintlock weapon designed by Ezekiel Baker using the same action as the smooth-bore Brown Bess infantry musket, but it had a shorter rifled barrel and a rear and foresight arrangement. It was considered too complex to issue to rank and file infantry, so a special unit was organised and the Rifle Brigade was raised. These were selected infantry, trained to fire the new weapon and make best use of its superior range and accuracy. The weapon was fitted with a sword bayonet, which made up for the lack of reach that the standard musket bayonet would have offered.

They wore green uniforms with black buttons which aided camouflage and were effectively used as skirmishing troops and what we now term as *snipers*. This flew in the face of the military traditionalists who still believed that troops should be highly visible and prepared to square up to and fight their enemies from close and intimidating musket range (up to about 100 yards) in the open and from square and ranked formations. The Rifle Brigade and their tactics were the future; they were lightly equipped and marched at 140 paces a minute, instead of the normal 120. The Baker rifle had an effective range of up to 300 yards, even further in very skilled hands and in calm conditions. Wellington used them in the Peninsular War and they are admirably represented in the TV series *Sharpe*, starring Sean Bean, and based on Bernard Cornwell's *Sharpe* series of novels.

The Rifle Brigade became the Royal Green Jackets in the 1950s but have since been disbanded. However, their proud traditions live on within the The Rifles battle group, which is an amalgamation of regiments that maintain strong links and uphold traditions associated with those early principles.

ℛOUNDS

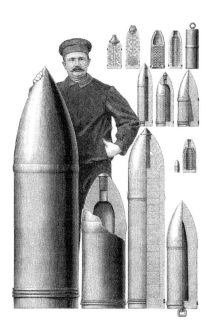

A predominantly military term for live cartridges.

Referring to the period when military muskets fired *round ball*, before the days of the more efficient conical bullets. Military ammunition is still referred to as *ball* for standard rifle ammunition, *tracer* (illuminated path/incendiary), *armour piercing* (tungsten tipped), *sniper* (ball rounds that have been individually inspected for consistency), or *link* (joined rounds on a disintegrating metal belt for automatic weapons).

RUNNING AMOK

Another descriptive term describing a tendency to display anger or physical clumsiness. It essentially means the same as 'Going ballistic' (see **Ballistic / Going ballistic** *on page 28) or 'Going postal' (see* **Going postal** *on page 86).*

The term *amok*, according to OED, means '*behave uncontrollably and disruptively*' and is derived from the Malay *amok* 'rushing in a frency'. Associated with displays of extremely violent and unprovoked attacks, often in a drug-induced frenzy, with victims being injured and even killed.

In South East Asian cultures it was considered that such a person had been possessed by the spirit of an evil tiger. Of course, the true issue is a state of mind associated with serious mental conditions and illness and that is not restricted to South East Asia.

RUN THE GAUNTLET / RUNNING THE GAUNTLET

Subjected to a series of verbal taunts and provoked exchanges. A competitive test. An intense physical challenge, even a manoeuvre in wartime, which anticipates high risk.

Considered to be a form of punishment linked to the training of soliders whereby subjects were directed to move between two lines of peers who would then strike with weapons, iron gloves, etc.

According to OED, *run the gauntlet* comes from Old French *gantelet*, *gant* 'glove' then alteration of this in Swedish *gatlopp*, from *gata* 'lane' + *lopp* 'course'.

Sabre-rattling

A demonstration of discontent and discord; a sign of provocation or pending action.

A more literal term associated with battle preparation and intimidation at the scene of battle or conflict. There is no defined origin to this, and no wonder when you consider how long edged weapons like the *sabre* have been in existence. The clashing of steel weapons and the beating of shields is a centuries-old tactic to intimidate an enemy prior to an attack. Even today, police and military forces trained in riot control utilise the tactic of beating their shields with batons.

A US Congressman called John F Miller, at a Congressional hearing on 21st February 1921, is said to have expressed his views on the threat of Japan's active militarism since World War I making reference to '*sabre rattling*'. It was regarded as a common figure of speech at the time.

There's also the famous event called *Ruido de sables* 'noise of sabers' in 1924 where a group of disgruntled soldiers literally *rattled sabres* in their scabbards (the sheath to hold the sabre). The event was a precursor to a military coup d'état overthrowing the Chilean political powers of the time.

The term is still applied to describe an indication of military strength or intent. Major military exercises and weapon tests, particularly nuclear weapon testing, can portray an explicit form of *sabre-rattling*. A country's military might is put on display for all to see. News reports suggest the Russian invasion of Ukraine in 2022 was preceded, initiated, conducted and continued in conjunction with President Vladimir Putin's endless *sabre-rattling*. The Russians, since the end of World War II, have become very adept and keen to display their military prowess in large and colourful military parades. Their performance in the field, however, doesn't appear to accurately represent it any longer.

Salvo

A very direct slant; overwhelmed with criticism; pertinent and directed declaration. Also used in the medical profession to describe monitored dysfunctional and irregular clustered heart beats.

This term is more usually associated with naval gunnery, a *salvo* being a concurrent firing of guns to either hit a target or to perform a military salute. The term is commonly used to describe the synchronised firing of cannon by warships.

In the dawn of the 17th century, guns aboard warships could fire in all directions, but reloading took time and it left the warship vulnerable to enemy return fire while the gunners reloaded. But, by 1640 the cannons on warships (or *ships of the line* as they were known) were arranged so they pointed out along each side of the vessel, as opposed to the bow or stern. In this arrangement, the canons, which could be reloaded quicker by that time anyway, could all be presented *broadside* (see **Broadside** on page 47) known as *the line of battle* and then fired in one devastating *salvo* and, crucially, without breaking the battle line and mistakenly firing upon a vessel of the same line.

Following the Crimean War, where vulnerabilities of wooden ships was identified, the first ironclads (steam-powered ships armoured with iron plates) were commissioned from 1843 by the British Admiralty. Over time these developed to have turreted guns fitted and the line of cannons phased out.

SITTING ON A POWDER KEG

Risking or prompting an unwanted or unwelcome outcome; foolishly exposing oneself.

Black *gunpowder* in bulk was stored and contained within barrels or containers. Whilst probably marked and covered, it would not have followed the more sophisticated process we now have for the storage of explosives and propellants. Black gunpowder is notoriously volatile; minimum exposure to flame or spark is easily sufficient to detonate it.

Modern firearm propellants have to be contained within a cartridge to be successfully detonated, expose it to flame in loose format and it simply burns. The same can be said of modern explosives. Initiation must be extremely contained and intense. A *keg* of gunpowder might have looked quite innocent but the risk of obliviously sitting on one and proceeding to charge and light a pipe, for instance, was highly dangerous.

SKINFLINT

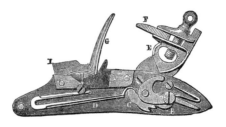

A person with a miserly disposition.

The specially cut *flint* held in the jaws of a flintlock

mechanism gradually wore down with use. To maximise shots from a worn flint the strike edge was carefully taped with a small hammer to burr it, thus creating an edge more likely to spark; this was apparently referred to as *skinning a flint*. A firer might try to maximise the use out of a flint, rather than just replace it with a new one at more expense. The same practise is referred to the flints in a tinder box.

Sharpshooter

A very general term referring to someone who is a very good shot with a rifle. Armed assailants at the scene of a successful assassination are often described by the common press in such a manner.

The term *scharfshutzen* 'sharpshooter' originated in Holland and in the German states in the 16th century. Men engaged in competitive shooting matches with smoothbore and rifled muskets prided themselves on achieving high degrees of accuracy. Riflemen raised and trained in *sharpshooter* techniques were deployed by Colonel Hiram Berdan, 1st Regiment Union Army during the American Civil War of 1860–1865.

They were eventually armed with the very strong and accurate breech-loading single-shot .52 calibre Sharps Rifle. By coincidence the name *Sharps* strengthened the association with long-range accuracy. The Sharps Rifle Company, founded by Christian Sharps, patented a new breech mechanism in 1848. The breech was exposed by cranking the trigger guard which was a hinged lever; this lowered the breechblock and exposed the chamber. The first models were loaded with paper cartridges which had the base scythed open when the breechblock was closed, thus exposing the gunpowder charge in the chamber. This was ignited by the detonation of a percussion cap. Later versions fired a self-contained metallic cartridge.

This powerful single-shot weapon became famous for its reliability, strength and range. Not only did the Sharps become synonymous with long-range shooting, but it was the favoured rifle of many of the buffalo hunters who ended up decimating herds of these beasts in the American West.

SHELL-SHOCKED

Surprised by the nature of an event or a verbal assault, from an emotional perspective. Not the outcome of a physical threat.

A term that came from observing the characteristics of some military personnel subjected to bombardment and gunfire during the First World War. Thought initially to be the physical result of blast-related concussion, loss of hearing and pressure. Later studies concluded that, whilst all these physical traumas would be relevant, there were deep-rooted psychological traumas also being manifested from intense fear, shock, dread and helplessness. As warfare and weapon delivery systems became more remote and potent into the 20th century and beyond, studies began to recognise the burdens suffered by those exposed to them. The term is now referred to as *PTSD*.

Shrapnel

Loose coins, or change, in our pocket.

Major General Henry *Shrapnel* (1761–1842) was a very innovative artillery officer in the British Army. He devised metal artillery casings that were designed to burst as an explosive, uniformly discharging muskets balls or deadly metal shards, which caused maximum damage to enemy troops in the open. Examples of his ordnance were used very successfully at the Battle of Waterloo. The term *shrapnel* later became synonymous with the fragmentation effects of grenades, artillery shells and bombs. The link with coins came about through slang used by the New Zealand military in the First World War.

SHOOT FROM THE HIP

The action of an opportunist making a quick decision, or a plan or proposal initiated before a final check. A person renowned for quick retorts.

Shooting from the hip probably derives from the action of drawing a holstered pistol and firing quickly at a target with the weapon at waist level rather than being brought up to aim at arm's length. In reality, probably infrequently practised, fanciful and over dramatized, but a tactic used in modern close-quarter battles with sub-machine guns.

141

Shoot first, ask questions later

A very established Americanism, referring to someone who wades into a scenario apportioning blame and responsibility without initially studying the context of a situation.

A rather crude literal practise associated with lawmen supposedly forced to act in a lawless and violent society in a manner to protect themselves from harm. Perhaps a

good example of where legend and reality clash. Undoubt-
edly and unfortunately, there will be examples where law
enforcement has acted in this manner.

SHOOTING BRAKE

*From the early 19th century a 'brake', or 'break', was a
simple four-wheeled carriage frame (chassis) with no body,
used for 'breaking in' and training young horses for harness
on private estates and away from the public roads.*

According to *Motor Body-Building In All Its Branches*
by C.W. Terry published back in 1914, where it carefully
describes different types of 'motor bodies', s*hooting brake*

is described as a type of waggonette, that is a carriage with seats running lengthways and usually with an entrance at the rear, sometimes doors at the side. However, the extra items added that defined it as a *shooting brake* were '*game and gun racks, and accommodation for ammunition.*'

Originating in the 1890s, these horse-drawn *shooting brakes* were loaded with a driver, gamekeeper and up to six others, where they would hunt game on large open estates. The concept evolved over time as horse-drawn carriages made way for automobiles, with Albion Motors of Scotland being an early pioneer manufacturer of *motorised shooting breaks.*

By 1930s, while some shooting break automobiles were being used to carry more modern hunting parties, like the 1931 Rolls-Royce Phantom Safari wagon, most where being used as a general car for commuting, travelling to get the shopping and going on holiday, so the term *estate car* was coined, as is now the definition in the OED.

However, the original term *shooting break* is still used by car manufacturers today to describe cars with features of estates, long bodies with four doors, or coupés, with two, and both styles normally having a sloped roofline extending past the rear wheels, over a large luggage space and rear door. In fact, Audi unveiled its '*Audi shooting break*' concept car at the 2005 Tokyo Motor Show and Mercedes-Benz produced a '*CLS Shooting Brake*' that went on sale in 2012.

Shot his bolt

A misjudgement; an ill-timed, last chance attempt.

The crossbow was a shoulder-held medieval weapon that was designed to fire a short arrow referred to as a *bolt*. It was a very powerful weapon and didn't demand as much skill and strength to operate as longbow, but it was more complicated to prepare and a lot slower to load. The firer always risked being exposed to an advancing enemy if he wasted a badly aimed shot; having *shot his bolt* to no effect he now had to face the hazardous task of a reload.

SHOT IN THE DARK

A chance approach, proposal or wager.

Referred to an un-aimed *shot* in the general direction of an enemy or quarry in *darkness*. In real terms, of course, this could be very dangerous, because it could result in fire being directed to friend as a well as foe. Friendly fire, or 'blue on blue' as the military term, is a consequence of the confusion that can result in warfare. There are examples of it occurring in every conflict and it can more easily happen at night.

Lieutenant John Chard RE, the Officer Commanding at Rorke's Drift during the famous action in the South African Anglo-Zulu War of 1879, was fired upon by inexperienced friendly troops. He was occupying a forward position near the Nondweni river when sentries in the main body behind him thought they were under attack and opened up an indiscriminate fire, wounding men and killing some horses.

Shot across the bows

Gefechtsordnung im Seegefecht bei Helgoland am 9. Mai 1864.

Heimdal.　Jylland.　Nils Juel.　　　Radetzky.　　Schwarzenberg.　Adler.　Basilisk. Blitz.

A verbal warning or directive.

An offensive naval tactic of firing a naval gun just in front of an opposing vessel's *bow* (the foremost part of the ship) as a warning. The advantage being simply that a well-placed *shot* will be clearly seen striking the sea in front of the vessel being warned or chased. This is effectively intimidating and threatening as the fall of shot is in plain view.

Shots

Spirits, liqueurs or short mixed drinks consumed in one go from short glasses in a celebratory fashion. Shot glasses are short spirit glasses with a heavy thickened base.

There are a number of stories supposedly linked to the term *shot*, that being the discharge of a firearm or gun. One military link has soldiers toasting an occasion then banging their glasses down on a table to replicate musket fire. Another is a glass positioned on a dining table for diners to deposit lead shot that they have found in the meat portions of their hunted game meals. Another description is a glass partly-filled with shot to accommodate and support writing quills. Also, an American western version of cow-boys paying for drinks with bullets. A vague suggestion is the association with Otto Schott, a German chemist who developed borosilicate glass. Schott was involved in the glass composition of optics rather than beverage glasses. Totally unclear, this one.

SHOTGUN

This term has not been adapted to mean anything else, but I had to include a section on this, because I refer to terminology we use to describe and associate with shotguns.

The most common reference you are likely to hear is the term *12 bore*. Now what exactly does that mean? If we have a lump of pure lead which weighs exactly one pound, divide it equally into twelve pieces then cast one of those amounts in a round bullet mould, producing a perfectly smooth round bullet, we have a munition that will fit the barrel diameter of a 12 bore.

This is a very old system of measurement or gauging, but this is how we arrive at these figures. The *shotgun* gauges we currently find now are 12, 16, 20, and 28 bore; the most common of which is 12. Therefore, the larger the figure, the smaller the bore diameter.

Americans prefer to use the term *gauge*, so they will, for instance, describe a *12 gauge*. We, on the other hand, generally use the term *bore*; both references mean exactly the same. The smallest shotgun gauge is .410, which is, of course, an imperial measurement. This one bucks the trend.

Shotgun wedding

A hastily arranged event that is not to everybody's taste.

This phrase is attributed to the American novelist Sinclair Lewis, appearing in his 1927 satirical novel *Elmer Gantry*. It refers to a quickly organised wedding in less tolerant days gone by. The father of the pregnant bride might have threatened the young man who is being forced and destined to become his son-in-law, thus making his daughter an 'honest' woman. The very thought of this prospective father-in-law attending the *wedding* armed with a *shotgun* is a preposterous thought.

SHOOT THE MESSENGER

Laying blame and directing scorn at the feet of a messenger or conveyancer who brings bad news.

In ancient times *killing a messenger* who conveyed bad news might have occurred on occasions. The messenger was often an innocent party who risked such action from an enraged recipient. The Greek playwright Sophocles, in an English translation of his play *Antigone*, writes a similar sentiment, '*Nobody likes the man who brings bad news.*' We liberally use the term now; setting out to impart bad news or unwanted rhetoric we meekly request that the recipients '*Don't shoot the messenger!*'

Shooting fish in a barrel

Something easily obtained or contained for procurement with little effort.

The action of *shooting fish in a barrel* conjures up an image of easy and pointless slaughter.

American journalist Gene Fowler uses the phrase ' "... *It's like shooting fish in a barrel...* "' in his 1935 book *The Great Mouthpiece: A Life Story of William J. Fallon*, but it was probably used long before that.

Shot to bits / Shot to pieces

A person that has been overwhelmingly upset or is hugely concerned or frightened, or something that is ruined. A hugely exaggerated form of terminology.

The gruesome scene of a person or animal that has suffered from multiple gunshot wounds, or an object or structure *shot* at, might indeed be literally as the idiom describes.

Shot down in flames

Winning an argument, debate or discussion against an individual adversary.

A rather overused and grossly exaggerated expression which is far removed from the horror of the reality: namely an aircraft being *shot down* and crippled and in an uncontrollable descent which will conclude with inevitable loss of life. The sight of an aircraft being destroyed in flight by a modern defence system (a surface-to-air or an air-to-air missile) is a shocking and mesmerising sight.

154

Smoking gun

Evidence at the scene of a wayward event or crime.

Could literally be as described at the scene of a murder or assassination: a *gun* that has just been fired. The phrase *the smoking gun* was first made famous when uttered by U.S. Congressman Barber B. Conable regarding the tape recording of Richard Nixon wishing to not have the FBI involved in the 1970s Watergate scandal. Later, the idiom *smoking gun* was much used in the controversy about the search for weapons of mass destruction and the prelude to war in Iraq in 2003.

Earlier guns used black gunpowder which when fired produced a lot of flame and *smoke*. This effluent could loiter; modern smokeless propellant, less so.

SMOKESCREEN

An action that deliberately conceals, confuses or obscures.
Often associated with unethical practises.

In military terms it is a tried and tested method of pre-
venting an enemy from seeing movement in the form of
an attack or a withdrawal. Only a few recorded examples
of this practice can be found prior to the First World War.
Smoke is released or generated to mask the movement or
location of military ground units, aircraft or warships.
On the ground it is most commonly deployed in a canis-
ter, usually as a grenade. Modern technology brings the
availability to screen in the infrared as well as the visible
spectrum to prevent detection by infrared sensors or view-
ers. There are super dense forms that disrupt enemy target
designators or rangefinder lasers. Simple methods utilised
boiled waste oil over a heater, while more sophisticated
ones sprayed a specially formulated oily composition of
fog oil through nozzles onto a heated plate. Warships have

sometimes used a simple variation of the smoke generator, by injecting fuel oil directly into the smokestack. They were used to great effect during the Second World War. In the Vietnam War *smoke ships* were introduced as part of a new air-mobile concept to protect crew and men on the ground from small arms fire.

There are a number of early examples of using incendiary weapons at sea such as Greek fire, a liquid charge mostly of naphtha. The original naval *smoke screen* is often said to have been proposed by Sir Thomas Cochrane in 1812, although Sir Cochrane's proposal was meant to asphyxiate as well as be an obscurant.

SNIPING

Delivering irritating criticism, or continual short derogatory accusations or comment, to someone.

The art and skill of the true weapon *sniper* is often misunderstood, and it is a grossly overused and abused reference even in shooting terms. It is a skill that requires physical endurance, immense patience, physical bravery and exceptional fieldcraft, navigation and shooting skills. A sniper is required to be able to kill specific targets whilst remaining completely unseen, often firing over long ranges using a minimal amount of ammunition. With no further support he will be expected to withdraw or move to another task unaided and undetected.

By the late 18th century the term *sniper* was being used to describe a *snipe shooter*. A *snipe* is a small fast-flying game bird, erratic in flight and a difficult target. To *go out sniping* and be successful was an accomplishment, especially with the flintlock weapons of that time. In strict military terms, soldiers who were particularly accomplished shots were referred to as *marksman* or *sharpshooters* (see **Sharpshooter** on page 137). It wasn't until the First World War that the term *sniper* reappeared, making reference to soldiers armed with rifles generally fitted with telescopic sights.

Social hand grenade

Generally describing a person lacking in social skills, empathy and understanding and likely to pass comment

and commit actions that might shock, offend and surprise, before thinking of the consequences.

A *hand grenade* is a small explosive device that can be thrown at a target. The weapon is armed, and the fuse is set when the firing lever initiates under spring tension when it is released. This can only occur after a retaining safety pin is removed. Hand grenades are devastating in confined spaces.

The pin is very securely in place and requires some effort to remove it. The Hollywood portrayal of a soldier removing a pin with their teeth is pure fantasy and fabrication.

Soldiering on / Solider on

The action of enduring either physical or mental stress in absolutely any situation.

Soldiering for those who have experienced it know only too well that this noble profession is 90% toil and 10% action. The physical determination and utter resilience of troops preceding a battle has in itself been sufficient to win it—moving over long distances in all conditions, carrying weapons and equipment, enduring hunger, thirst, anxiety, pain and fear. In peacetime, only endurance sports come mildly close in comparison.

SON OF A GUN

An affectionately or kindly regarded type of person, a liked and lucky character, or a term used as an interjection expressing surprise, mild annoyance or disappointment.

Apparently, in Royal Naval slang this term was used by crew on lower deck that referred to a child being born on board a warship. It is sometimes claimed that the saying has its origin in the supposed practice of women embarked on ships and giving birth on a sectioned-off portion of the gun deck to keep the main gangways clear. Admiral William Henry Smyth wrote in his 1867 book, *The Sailor's Word-Book*, *'An epithet conveying contempt in a slight degree, and originally applied to boys born afloat, when women were permitted to accompany their husbands to sea; one admiral declared he literally was thus cradled, under the breast of a gun-carriage.'*

In American folklore this term has a similar meaning but was derived from the military approach to young, enlisted men of uncertain background. If a recruit was unable to state his father's name officers supposedly recorded *'A Gun'*. *Cambridge Advanced Learner's Dictionary* and *Webster's Dictionary* both define *son of a gun* as a term in American English as *'a euphemism for son of a bitch'*.

SPIKING GUNS / TO SPIKE A GUN

To hold up; interfere (to spike their guns); jeopardise; trash a plan, objective or process.

Muzzle-loaded artillery could be quickly disabled by driving or hammering a steel or iron *spike* into the touchhole, thus blocking passage to fire a charge. Triangular bayonets could be utilised for this task. Disabling captured enemy *guns* that could not be taken away was an option to deny further use. Artillery units forced to retire or withdraw without their guns might *spike* their own pieces to deny enemy use of them.

STARING DOWN THE BARREL (OF A GUN)

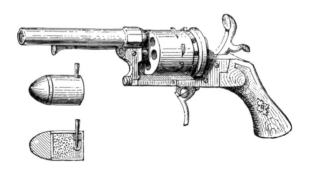

Impending doom or dramatic change; anticipating and facing failure, disaster or danger in any context.

The very instance and experience of facing the muzzle of a *gun barrel* pointed at you is one of intense, personal and ultimate threat.

STICK TO YOUR GUNS

Holding on to your beliefs, rights and convictions.

The term is considered to be military in origin. Author Christine Ammer writes in her 1990 book *Fighting Words: From War, Rebellion, and Other Combative Capers*, '... *Less in doubt than managing to hit a target was a gunner's obligation to stay at his post, whence the British term "stand to one's guns" (in America, "stick to one's guns"), meaning to persist and not give way...*' This is to be more associated with gun crews working with artillery who are reluctant to run from the field of battle and desert their sacred field guns.

According to the same author, a 1909 newspaper article about members of known pacifists the Society of Friends reported this: '*"The Quakers stood to their guns, and, without any resort to brute force, finally won."*'

Oh, the irony.

TAKE A SHOT / TAKE THE SHOT

In ball sports, especially football; have a go at something; to launch a difficult question or be seen to verbally attacking someone in front of others.

To take the opportunity for a *shot* at a target. A sniper, after some consideration, would *take a shot* when the best opportunity or circumstance was offered.

TAKING A BULLET

A member of an organisation or corporate team taking

the full force of criticism that might have been directed at a more senior figure.

The near suicidal or sacrificial action of *taking a bullet* to protect another person might reflect a similar approach but in a literal fashion. Official security teams and individuals assigned to the personal protection of political figures have placed themselves between assailants and assassins intent on causing harm or killing dignitaries. On occasions throughout history, bodyguards have *taken a bullet* or blow actually meant for the very person they are protecting.

𝒯ANK

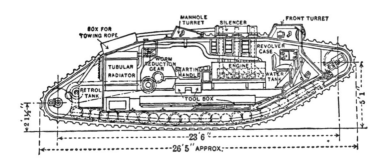

Something, often a vehicle, or somebody described as being 'built like a tank', inferring great strength and resilience. Also, to describe something failing in a spectacular

*way, often used in connection with a Hollywood movie
not being a box-office success.*

This is a well-used simile, but the origin of the name *tank*
(an armoured, tracked fighting vehicle) originated during
the First World War when the word was first applied to
describe these vehicles in 1915. Before they entered service
it was important to keep their nature secret and there are
a number of explanations that suggest how they were so
called. The hulls of these vehicles looked like huge water
tanks and construction staff were given the impression they
were constructing mobile water tanks for the British Army.

A consignment was planned for the Russians who were
going to receive 'water carriers'. When a secret report on
the new weapon was presented to Winston Churchill,
then First Lord of the Admiralty, by British Army Lt. Col.
Ernest Swinton, three descriptive terms emerged: *cistern*,
motor-war car and *tank*. Simplicity would seem to have
settled with *tank*. In Germany tanks are usually referred
to as *panzers* 'armour', a shortened version of the full
term *panzerkampfwagen*, which literally means 'armoured
fighting vehicle'. The term *panzer* has since ironically been
unofficially adopted by British armoured units to describe
their own machines. That might be as a result of the rapid
advance in tank technology that the Germans made during
the Second World War and the respect bestowed on them
by their allied adversaries.

TIME BOMB

A person so described having a short temper, or a violent person who is prone to lose control of themselves; a situation that may become serious.

An explosive device set to detonate at a prescribed time by the utilisation of a *timer* or fuse. The physiological effect of a *time bomb* (or delayed action device) can be overwhelming, and the fear of these devices can cause maximum disruption and panic. There was much use of these type of weapons during World War II by all sides, and it has become a favoured method utilised by terrorist groups.

TO RAM IT HOME

To forcefully make a point to someone.

Refers to the assertive and determined action of loading a muzzle-loading firearm or artillery piece with a *ramrod*. This process required a measured charge of gunpowder, wadding and the projectile to be introduced at the muzzle end of a weapon and then *rammed* down the entire barrel length to the breech. The introduction of paper cartridges for use by troops simplified and accelerated the loading process.

TO HAVE A BEAD ON SOMEONE

To be observing somebody of interest or an adversary, possibly looking for a weakness.

Refers to the simple *bead* foresight generally found at the muzzle end of a shotgun barrel. The shorter range of a shotgun and the target, often moving, requires the firer to align the weapon using the *bead* sight while keeping both eyes open.

𝒯ORPEDO

To jeopardise, compromise, ruin, demotivate.

An underwater, cigar-shaped, self-propelled explosive device designed to damage or destroy seaborne vessels, launched from submarine or aircraft. A ship sunk as a result of *torpedoes* is a devastating sight and thus the term is used in an exaggerated context to emphasise extent and feeling.

According to OED, the word *torpedo* also is the name of an electric ray, the *torpedo ray*, the name originating from Latin meaning 'stiffness, numbness' and by connection the electric ray can causes these symptoms, from *torpere* 'be numb or sluggish'.

169

The American maritime inventor Robert Fulton was a proponent of *torpedoes* and some writers say he appropriated the name for his experiments with sea mines (explosive charges moored at sea), and the name *torpedo* followed to also mean a mine dragged by a rope or fired with harpoon, and also explosive devices called *spar torpedoes* attached to poles extending from the bow of small boats, but the modern *self-propelled torpedo* we think of today was invented by British engineer Robert Whitehead in 1866.

'TWO, SIX'

A predominately Naval term meaning a standby command prior to a body of persons about to use their combined strength to move a heavy object.

From the order given to numbers *two* and *six* in a naval gun crew hauling ropes to move a muzzle-loading cannon to its firing or loading position (see **Broadside** on page 47) and (see **Salvo** on page 134).

𝒯O SHOOT ONESELF IN THE FOOT

To make a gross error of judgement and suffer as a result.

The result of a negligent discharge with a loaded firearm. The muzzle of any loaded firearm should always be pointed in a safe direction. In a confined space this is often straight down. Mishandling the mechanism, whilst possibly safeguarding others around, might result in an injury to a *foot* or lower limb.

When Paratroopers and Royal Marines landed at San Carlos from landing craft at the start of the conflict in the Falkland Islands in 1982 a single *shot* rang out as one of the craft beached causing hundreds of troops, with already frayed nerves, to assume the worst. This was, in fact, just one soldier negligently discharging his weapon (a 9mm Sterling sub-machine gun), sending the bullet through part of his boot, his *foot* and into the vessel's deck. He was lucky to escape serious injury and received no thanks from the rest of the assaulting troops. A negligent discharge (ND) in the armed forces is considered as a serious misdemeanour and in peacetime it is a chargeable offence.

*T*RIGGER / *P*ULLING THE TRIGGER

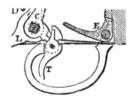

To start or initiate something. 'Pulling the trigger' is a term used in sport, rugby being a good example. This is when a player, poised and in possession of the ball, sees an opportunity and route to run for the touchline to score.

The very action of discharging a firearm is by pulling back (referred to as *squeezing*) a protruding curved lever, the *trigger*, on the underside of the weapon. From the Dutch, *trekken* 'to pull'.

TRIGGER-HAPPY

Keen or overzealous.

The action of someone discharging a firearm in an undisciplined manner. Delivering shots indiscriminately before assessing a target.

TRIGGER FINGER

Direct reference to a forefinger, usually the right.

A reference to anatomy merely as an indicator, but with no suggestion in a literal sense. Most people are right-handed and thus hold a firearm in a manner that enables them to use their right forefinger on a *trigger*.

Volley

A noisy, quick emission of oaths or protestations. A directly returned ball in football or tennis with no bounce; Volleyball, a ball game dependent on handing or punching a ball with no hold or bounce.

From the French *volée*, originally from Latin *volare* 'to fly'. In a military context, meaning *sustained gunfire*. In the days of single-shot firearms, troops were trained in *volley fire* whereby they fired together in ranks under strict orders and discipline in order to deliver a heavy, continuous and devastating weight of fire.

WARPAINT

A term describing a person's facial makeup.

Generally associated with indigenous, tribal warrior races throughout the world. The act of applying colour to their faces and bodies was to intimidate their enemies and provide them with strengths and powers. Native American Indians were great advocates of this style of decoration, the term *warpaint*, given of course by their so-called 'civilised' enemies. Similarly, many African tribes decorated their faces and bodies with paint before battle to intimidate their enemy.

Interestingly, another term that I became accustomed to during my time in the military was that of a female's *fighting order*. A fighting order, in pure military terms, is the equipment worn by a soldier which is attached to a belt and shoulder yoke, such as ammunition pouches, water, rations, survival equipment, etc. The fighting order stays on the soldier while the bergen (rucksack used by the military) can be discarded. A female's fighting order also consisted of her choice of evening attire and paid particular attention to the arrangement and choice of underwear. Therefore, a young soldier referring to or describing a female 'wearing her warpaint and fighting order' was never being derogatory, he was, in fact, being wholly complimentary.

Went off at half cock / Going off at half cock / At half cock / Half-cock

A plan, statement or action that has been prematurely executed or initiated.

A flintlock or percussion firearm had a *half and full cock* position for the hammer. The *full cock* position was engaged to fire, the hammer being held back by a very strong spring and released by pulling the trigger. The *half cock* position was to give the firer access to the flash pan, cap nipple or release the spring tension on a firing pin to open a breech action. It also allowed the weapon to be inspected for cleanliness or safety. The weapon could not be fired, because this was a safe position. A faulty sear spring, however, might allow the hammer to fall if the trigger was pulled and thus result in a negligent, unplanned, and possibly dangerous, discharge.

The order '*Half-cock!*' existed as a firearms drill term. In the military, the order '*Ease springs!*' is given to release the held tension on the hammer thus allowing it to rest harmlessly and safely in its fully forward position. The term is still used today and applies in exactly the same way to a hammer or sprung firing mechanism, which ultimately is designed to drive a firing pin forward under released spring tension.

WHEN THE BALLOON GOES UP

The implication of possible or impending trouble.

This is largely considered to relate to the use of tethered observation *balloons* during the First World War. Helium-filled balloons were launched to enable military observers to study enemy troop dispositions (their arrangement ready for battle) and movement, and direct and correct artillery fire onto them. The sight of such a balloon going up was therefore the precursor to an artillery barrage, which might result in counterfire from the enemy. The expression continued during World War II when anti-aircraft weapons were launched as part of the defensive preparations to combat and interfere with an adversary's air raids. These balloons were unmanned and attached to strong steel cables. The idea was to dissuade enemy aircraft from flying low over targets which might have enabled them to bomb more accurately. Hot-air observation balloons were used as early as the American Civil War (1861–1865).

(THE) WHOLE NINE YARDS

An expression relating to the sum total of anything.

Lots of conjecture about this well-worn expression; a wealth of options and no clear origin. Best research suggests it started to be used around the 1960s. It has been linked to various originations including the length of bomb racks aboard US bombers, the length of machine gun ammunition belts fitted to certain types of World War II aircraft and the length of ammunition belts in ground-based anti-aircraft turrets.

A naval reference is another theory. The spars (cross members on a mast) or *yards*, as they were also described, being the link here. When an enemy vessel was changing direction in battle the choice of sails was closely monitored. The selection of sail on the *ninth yard* inferred an intended course. This theory is dubious if you consider that by the 1960s, sailing ships would have fallen out of use.

Other popular theories suggest a medieval test requiring the victim to walk *nine paces* over hot coals, and tailors supposedly use *nine yards* of material to construct top quality suits, related to the expression *dressed to the nines*.

So what is the truth? I'll leave the last word to author and etymology enthusiast Michael Quinion who writes in his 2004 book *Port Out, Starboard Home and Other Language Myths*, '*I feel that, failing the discovery of the lexicographical equivalent of the crock of gold at the end of the rainbow, we are unlikely to find the truth about this one.*'

BIBLIOGRAPHY & REFERENCES

Books, eBooks and Other Publications

Ammer, Christine. 1990. *Fighting Words: From War, Rebellion, and Other Combative Capers*. Dell Pub Co.

Bottomley, Frank. 1979. *The Castle Explorer's Guide*. Kaye & Ward Ltd.

Brock, Alan St. H. 1922. *Pyrotechnics: The History and Art of Firework Making*. Daniel O'Connor.

Brookes, Ian (editor). 2018. *Collins English Dictionary*. 13th edition. Collins.

Dunkling, Leslie. 1998. *Dictionary of Curious Phrases*. HarperCollins Publishers.

Finlason, W. F. 1880 – . *Reeves' History of the English Law, From the Romans to the End of the Reign of Elizabeth*. M Murphy.

Fleming, James S. 2004. *Window on Congress: A*

Congressional Biography of Barber B. Conable, Jr. University of Rochester Press.

Fraser, Edward. 1913. *The Soldiers Whom Wellington Led: Deeds of Daring, Chivalry, and Renown.* Methuen.

Fulton, Robert. 1810. *Torpedo War and Submarine Explosions.* William Elliot.

Guderian, Heinz. 2012. *Achtung-Panzer! The Development of Tank Warfare.* Orion.

Gulland, Daphne M & David Hinds-Howell. 1994. *The Penguin Dictionary of English Idioms 2nd Edition.* Penguin Books.

Humphreys, Col. David. 1818. *An Essay on the Life of the Honourable Major General Israel Putnam.* Samuel Avery.

Jack, Albert. 2005. *Shaggy Dogs and Black Sheep: The Origins of Even More Phrases We Use Every Day.* Penguin Books.

Keegan, John. 1995. *Warpaths: Travels of a Military Historian in North America.* Random House.

Kemp, Peter (editor). 1990. *The Oxford Companion to*

Ships and the Sea. Oxford University Press.

Lavery, Brian. 2004. *Ship: 5,000 Years of Maritime Adventure*. Dorling Kindersley.

Milner, N. P. (translator). 2001. *Vegetius: Epitome of Military Science*. Liverpool University Press.

Partridge, Eric. 1933. *Word, Words, Words!* Taylor & Francis.

Peck, Colin. 2008. *British Woodies: From the 1920's to the 1950's*. Veloce Publishing.

Pegler, Martin. 2004. *Out of Nowhere: A History of the Military Sniper*. Osprey Publishing.

Peterson, Harold L. and Robert Elman. 1971. *The Great Guns*. Hamlyn Publishing.

Quinion, Michael. 2004. *Port Out, Starboard Home and Other Language Myths*. Penguin Books.

Robinson, Tony (forward). *Bloody Britain: A history of murder, mayhem and massacre*. AA Publishing.

Smyth, Admiral W. H. 1867. *The Sailor's World-Book: An*

Alphabetical Digets of Nautical Terms. Blackie and Son.

Speake, Jennifer (editor). 1999. *Oxford Dictionary of Idioms.* Oxford University Press.

Stevenson, Angus. 2010. *The Oxford English Dictionary,* Third Edition. Oxford University Press.

Terry, C. W. 1914. *Motor Body-Building In All Its Branches.* E. & F. N. Spon, Limited.

Wilkinson, Fred. 1977. *The World's Greatest Guns.* Hamlyn publishing.

Willmott, H.P. , Robin Cross, Charles Messenger and Various. 2004. *World War II.* Dorling Kindersley.

Author unknown. 1848. *Instruction Upon the Art of Pointing Cannon, For The Use of Young Sea Officers.* J and G. S. Gideon.

Various authors. 2007. *The Origins of Words & Phrases.* Reader's Digest.

Web and Other Resources

Wikipedia.org

History.co.uk

HistoryWorld.net

TheViolenceProject.org

GreensDictOfSlang.com

Parmoor Clay Shooting Club.

*I*ndex of *T*erms

T

V

Lightning Source UK Ltd.
Milton Keynes UK
UKHW021546080922
408529UK00006B/122